# MORAL
# QUESTIONS

**Is there a Christian attitude to abortion?
Should a Christian take part in strikes?
Should I care about the Third World?
Many Christians are worried by these and
other similar problems. This book does not
claim to have the definitive answers, but it
does set out in concise form the attitudes
and teachings of the Bible. Its contributors
are experts in their own fields and provide
interesting insights into these moral
questions. They might even raise more!**

# MORAL
# QUESTIONS

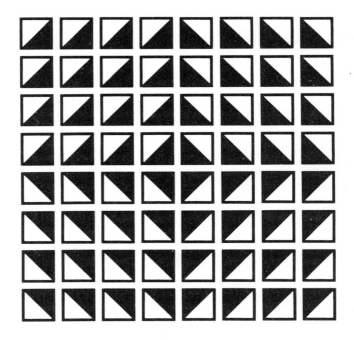

A discussion of Christian
attitudes to some thirty-five
social issues, edited by
CANON FRANK COLQUHOUN

**◪FALCON**

A FALCON BOOK

*published by*
Church Pastoral Aid Society
Falcon Court, 32 Fleet Street, London, EC4Y 1DB

*distributed overseas by*
Australia: Emu Book Agencies Ltd, 63 Berry Street, Granville, NSW 2142
Canada: The Book Society of Canada, PO Box 200, Agincourt, Ontario
New Zealand: Scripture Union Wholesale, PO Box 760, Wellington
Singapore State: SU Christian Book Centre, 36H Prinsep Street, Singapore
South Africa: SUBASA, 83 Camp Ground Road, Rondebosch 7700,
Cape Town

# MORAL
# QUESTIONS

ISBN 0 85491 854 X
First published 1977
Text © CPAS 1977

DESIGNED AND PRODUCED IN THE UNITED KINGDOM
*photoset in Baskerville type and bound by*
Richard Clay (The Chaucer Press) Ltd, Bungay, Suffolk
*printed offset litho by*
Fletcher & Son Ltd, Norwich, Norfolk

# contributors

Richard Ablitt
Joyce G. Baldwin BA BD
Professor R. J. Berry MA PhD
The Rev. Richard Bewes MA
The Most Rev. and Rt Hon. Stuart Blanch,
   Archbishop of York
The Rev. Dr Colin Brown MA PhD
Eunice R. Burton MB BS FRCS MRCOG
The Rev. Maurice C. Burrell MA
John Capon
Sir Frederick Catherwood DSc
The Rev. Julian Charley MA
The Rev. Canon Frank Colquhoun MA
James C. P. Cowley
Frank Deeks
D. Ruth Etchells MA BD
The Rev. David Field MA
Elizabeth S. Gardner LRCP LRCS
The Rev. R. F. R. Gardner LRCP LRCS FRCOG
Eddie Gibbs
Martin F. Goldsmith MA
The Rev. Dr Walter P. Hedgcock MD BS MRCS MRCGP
Garth Hewitt BA
The Rev. George Hoffman MA
O. R. Johnston MA
The Rev. Derek Kidner MA
Deaconess Una Kroll MB BChir MRCGP
Professor Basil Mitchell MA
The Rev. Dr J. I. Packer MA DPhil
The Rt Rev. C. Kenneth Sansbury MA DD
The Rev. Michael Saward BA
The Rev. Eddie Stride
The Ven. John B. Taylor MA
The Rev. Alan Wagstaff
The Rev. Canon M. A. C. Warren MA DD

# contents

# contents...

# Editor's Preface

This book is intended to serve as a companion to the symposium *Hard Questions*, first published in 1967 and recently reissued in a revised edition. That work concentrates on matters of Christian doctrine and deals largely with theological problems. The present work has a different emphasis. It is concerned in the main with ethical issues, particularly with those that confront us in our present society and which Christians are obliged to face and resolve in the light of their faith.

Most of the questions raised are large ones and of a complex character. Certainly many of them do not permit of a simple, cut-and-dried answer from the Christian viewpoint, nor is it possible to deal with them adequately or satisfactorily within a short compass. For that reason I am all the more grateful to those who have shared with me in this task and have contributed chapters. The directive they were given at the outset was that they should try to present both sides of the question and to offer some positive and practical guidance in accordance with Christian and biblical teaching.

Within that broad framework they had freedom to tackle their subject in whatever way they deemed best. There has been no collaboration between them, and they alone are responsible for the views they have expressed. The fact that they represent a certain diversity of stand-point and have adopted different approaches is inevitable in a symposium of this kind which ranges over so wide a field. But this at least can be said: all contributors have attempted to answer the questions posed to them in a fair and honest manner, with deep understanding of the various factors involved; and in the process they have shown that Christians are prepared to come to grips with these difficult issues of our time – and that they have something worthwhile to say about them.

A symposium is not an easy book to edit, or to produce; and so I end this preface by expressing my thanks to the Rev. Robert Backhouse, and Miss Eileen Thompson of Falcon Books for the patience they have exercised and for all the help they have given in getting the book into print.

*Norwich Cathedral*                                                    **Frank Colquhoun**

# I

# Can't you lead a decent life without being religious?

One approach to this question would be to turn it round and to ask, 'Can't you be religious without leading a decent life?' The answer of course is 'No.' Probably everyone would agree to that. All genuine religion has a strongly ethical character and demands certain standards of conduct. And that is certainly true of the Christian religion which claims to be not only a way of salvation but also a way of life.

The point I am making now at the outset of this introductory chapter is the intimate connection between religion and morality. The two are in fact inseparable. The living of a decent life is not something separate from religion. It is a vital part of religion.

This is not the place to discuss at length the anomaly of what is called the 'good pagan.' Admittedly there are many honourable and decent living people who never go to church or make an outward profession of religion. But it would be rash to conclude that they are necessarily irreligious or have no place for God in their lives. In fact their lives may be deeply coloured (whether they realise it or not) by religious influences in their family background as well as in their society. Who can tell? As Lord Inman stated a good many years ago, there must be multitudes of men and women who keep their religious convictions to themselves but who live outwardly decent lives because of those inner convictions.

At any rate, religious issues are involved as soon as we begin to think about the good life. This becomes clear when we look at these three questions.

First, what do we understand by the good life?
Second, why should we attempt to live it?
Third, how in fact can we do so?

In answering those questions we shall see that to live the good life we need direction, motive and power. And all these elements are made available to us in the religion of Jesus Christ, if only we are prepared to accept his claims and commit ourselves to him.

## Direction

What is meant by the good life? How are we to define it or assess it? Are there any absolute standards according to which we ought to live, or do we simply follow the highest and best as we see it?

It is at this point that the Christian faith offers us direction. It assures us that in making moral judgements – that is, in establishing what is 'good' – we are not left to our own human intuition or intelligence, or to the voice of conscience, or to the wisdom of the world. It points us to *God* who is the source of all goodness and who has made known his will for our lives in Jesus Christ. This is what we mean when we say that Christianity is a religion of revelation. That revelation is centred in Jesus Christ, the living Word, and embodied in the Bible, the written Word. Here we find out guidelines to the good life, the life that is in accordance with God's will.

Let us be clear that as Christians we do need direction about the way we are to live. Just because we are Jesus's disciples we do not pretend that we know the answers to all the baffling moral questions that confront us in life. And let us be clear too that the Bible does not provide ready-made solutions to all these problems. The Bible is more concerned with principles of living than with actual rules; and the primary principle is *love*. Love is the fulfilling of the law of Christ, for love is selfless, seeks the good of others, and makes sacrifices on their behalf. The parable of the good Samaritan in Luke 10:29–37 illustrates this, while St Paul's description of love (*agape*) in 1 Corinthians 13 provides the perfect portrait.

## Motive

This at once brings us to the next question and the matter of motive. *Why* should we live the good life? Why not please ourselves rather than put others first? To put it bluntly, why should we bother to love our neighbour?

The Christian answer is clear. We love our neighbour not simply because we are commanded to do so, or because this is what Jesus did – though these are two valid and compelling reasons. We love our neighbour *out of love for God*. This is where it all begins. Love of our neighbour is not the first commandment. It is the second. The first is to love God with our whole being; and the second arises out of that. For to love God is, among other things, to be grateful to him for all that he has given us, all that he has done for us – yes, and for all that he has suffered for us – and to act accordingly.

So in the end the cross is the supreme motive for Christian living. We are eternally in debt to Christ, and the only way we can discharge that debt is by loving and serving our fellow men. We love because he first loved us. We give ourselves in service because the Lord gave himself for us. We forgive others because God for Christ's sake has forgiven us. When the gospel of God's love really takes hold of us, it lifts us out of our narrow self-centred existence and gives to our lives a new moral impulse, a strong concern for others.

## Power

There remains the question of *how* we can actually do the things that as Christians we know we ought to do and want to do. It is not easy, even with the best will in the world. Clearly we need more than a moral urge if we are to follow the path of love, selflessness and service. We need also a moral *power*, a strength beyond our own – for we have no power of ourselves to help ourselves.

That power is also part of our inheritance in Christ. The gospel does not taunt us by setting before us some impossibly high ideal and then leave us to our own devices as to how to attain it. It promises us God's all-sufficient grace: the grace of the living Spirit of Christ dwelling in us to transform our lives, to renew our strength, to give us the victory over the forces of evil in ourselves and in the world.

Here is the secret of all moral achievement. 'I have strength for anything through him who gives me power,' testified St Paul out of his own experience (Philippians 4:13). The really distinctive thing about the Christian life is that Christ is not only our teacher, our pattern, our inspiration. He is also our enabler, our defender, our companion. Professor T. W. Manson summed it up in his book *Ethics and the Gospel*: 'The living Christ still has two hands, one to point the way, and the other held out to help us along. So the Christian ideal lies before us, not as a remote and austere mountain peak, an ethical Everest which we must scale by our own skill and endurance; but as a road on which we may walk with Christ as guide and friend.'

**Frank Colquhoun**

**Further reading**
*Consistent Christianity* Michael C. Griffiths (IVP)
*Free to do Right* David Field (IVP)
*Issues of life and death* Norman Anderson (Hodder & Stoughton)

# 2

# Do we need the Bible as a guide book in making moral judgements?

Making moral judgements in today's world is far from easy. The complexities of modern life can make moral decision-making about as intricate a business as picking a route through the crowded streets of a large city. Add the fact that many of these decisions have to be taken on the spur of the moment, and clear moral sign-posts become essential. So where are we to find them?

The answer that springs most easily to the Christian's mind is 'in the Bible.' The Bible is God's Word. As Christians, we believe that God still speaks to us through its pages. It is to the Bible, therefore, that we turn first for guidance in the moral problems we meet.

Natural and right though this approach is, we soon find that the Bible does not provide us with clear answers to all the questions we want to ask about morality. The Christian who pins his faith in the Scriptures as an 'Enquire within on everything' will certainly find some of his moral queries cleared up immediately. But in other cases the solutions may not be quite so obvious. In fact, there are three main grounds on which the Bible's usefulness as a moral guide-book has been challenged by its critics.

## Three Charges

● *It is out of date*
No one in his right mind would borrow a nineteenth-century road

map to find his way through a twentieth-century network of trunk roads and motorways. How, then, can it be right to rely for moral guidance on a book that is not just one hundred but nearly two thousand years old?

If we protest that the Bible is inspired by God – and he is every bit as alive today as he was in Old Testament time – we still have to reckon with the possibility that not all the rules and guidelines he laid down for people in Bible times are meant to apply to us today. The Bible talks about seething kids in their mother's milk and wearing hats in church (Exodus 23:19; 1 Corinthians 11:5) – the kind of issues which leave most twentieth-century readers puzzled, if not faintly amused.

### ● *It is inadequate*

When it comes to identifying the Bible's teaching on a particular subject, a concordance is a very useful tool. But no concordance contain words like 'strike,' 'euthanasia,' 'pill,' 'abortion' or 'H-bomb.' On these and many other moral issues which make the headlines in today's papers, the Bible is apparently silent.

Even on themes which Scripture does highlight, its teaching is not always immediately relevant to the specific issues modern people face. The Old Testament, for example, encourages large families and demands capital punishment for rebellious teen-agers (Genesis 1:28, 24:60; Psalm 127:4–5; Deuteronomy 21:18–21). Though such rules and guidelines might have been considered right for an underpopulated world where there were few means for dealing with violent social misfits, it is not nearly so obvious that they provide adequate guidance for Christians making their minds up on family planning and the death penalty today.

### ● *It is unnecessary*

In his letter to the Romans, Paul writes about people who do not read their Bibles but who still have moral standards and principles. Even those who live without the guidance of God's *written* law, he says, have that law 'written on their *hearts*' (Romans 2:15).

Modern life provides ample evidence that Paul was right. There are plenty of people without a vestige of Christian faith who fight racial discrimination, carry banners in anti-abortion marches, deplore pornography and are outraged by mugging. You do not have to be a regular Bible reader to have standards. So why do we need the

Bible to give us moral guidance, when we all have this inbuilt (and Christians would say 'God-given') sense of right and wrong anyway?

The criticisms sound plausible enough. But each has a compelling answer.

## We need the Bible

● *Because it clears our moral vision*
It is true that everyone has a sense of right and wrong. But, even in the best of us, that inbuilt moral sense has been blurred and distorted by sin. If we want to do something badly enough, our minds will convince us that black is white. If we do it often enough, even our consciences will stop giving out their warning signals. Making moral judgements unaided is like insisting on driving up a busy motorway at high speed with a misted up windscreen.

The Bible is God's own demister. It answers the most basic questions anyone can ask about morality: '*What is good?*' and '*What is right?*'

*Good* qualities, according to the Bible, are those we see reflected in God's character (Mark 10:18). For example if we are tempted to think that hoarding, or putting our own interests first, are not altogether bad traits, one glance at God's character as the Bible reveals it to us will be enough to set us back on course. And the *right* thing to do, according to the Bible, is always the thing that is in line with God's will (Romans 12:2; Hebrews 13:21). As we read the Scriptures, we are constantly pointed to the line God's will takes in small things as well as big, and these pointers sign-post us to right moral judgements in our own lives.

We need the Bible as a ship's captain needs his radar in a sea fog. To pretend that it is unnecessary is as stupid and as dangerous as it would be for an airline pilot to switch off his automatic systems and communications with the control tower as he comes in to land in poor visibility.

● *Because it points us to main-line principles*
It is true that the Bible does not offer made-to-measure solutions for every moral dilemma. But it does set out to achieve something far more important.

Every contemporary moral issue raises fundamental questions of right and wrong which sometimes lurk just below the surface. The abortion debate, for example, is not just about back-street operators and clinic touts at London Airport. It is about much more basic things – like the rights of the foetus, the true nature of compassion, and the sanctity of human life. And on these bed-rock matters the Bible has plenty to say and many clear directives to give.

To criticise the Scriptures as inadequate then, just because they do not include the vocabulary of the modern media, is far too shallow a reaction. The absence of the jargon forces us to look for the really big issues that lie below the surface of contemporary debate. And to be made to dig down to that foundation level is a very healthy antidote to hasty decision-making. The Bible stimulates us to work out moral judgements that are really sound – because they are based on main-line principles.

In much the same way it is short-sighted to discard the Bible as a guidebook just because, on those occasions when it *is* specific, it sometimes deals with problems that are no longer of much concern. Underlying every one of the specific directives Scripture offers is a main-line principle that is as relevant today as it ever was. For instance, behind the law on building roof-parapets (Deuteronomy 22:8) lies the principle of public safety. And the ban on seething a kid in its mother's milk illustrates the respectful attitude men should have at all times towards animals. Here we have main-line principles which have very clear applications to life today.

To make these claims is not just to counter the charge that the Bible's teaching is inadequate and outdated. To find adequate solutions to modern moral issues it is essential to distinguish the main principles at stake. And the Bible serves as a unique contemporary guide book simply because it directs us to those principles and gives us God's mind on them.

● *Because it directs us to the source of moral power*

In any moral dilemma, making the right decision is only stage one. Stage two – carrying the decision into practice – is much harder. For example, we do not really need anyone to tell us that generosity is right and bad-temperedness wrong; but in practice we know we are sometimes stingy and occasionally lose our temper. In other words, we lack the will-power to carry through the decisions we make quite sensibly in our minds.

At this level the Bible offers us a unique source of help. Some books on morality will convince us that we ought to live better lives. A few may even inspire us to make greater efforts. But in pointing us to the almighty God the Scriptures do far more than that. They direct us to a source of moral power which can overcome our weakness and make us free to do the right thing as well as avoid the wrong. Some people caricature the Bible as a book which is full of 'Thou shalt nots.' That is unfair. In fact, its central message is a triumphant 'You *can* – in God's power' (Philippians 4:13).

So the Bible is more than a guide book. It is God's power tool. Reading it regularly and obediently is like living with a piece of radio-active material in your pocket – though rather more healthy! Through the Scriptures God can break habits, change attitudes and reinforce wills (Philippians 2:13).

Over and above information and discernment in making moral judgements, we badly lack this power to make our decisions effective. The Bible directs us to the power source we need to convert our good intentions into action. There is no more cogent argument to drive us back to the Bible as our uniquely relevant, adequate and necessary guide in living the moral life.

**David Field**

**Further reading**
*Ethics in a Permissive Society* William Barclay (Fontana)
*The Way we Care* Gilbert Kirby (Scripture Union)
*Taking Sides* David Field (IVP)

# 3
# Should we always obey those in authority?

'Authority,' like 'love,' is a much misused word. People tend to make it mean what they want it to mean. Before we can consider whether we should always obey those in authority, therefore, we need to be clear about what we mean by authority.

My working definition is this: authority is power exercised legitimately.

As you will later see, such authority stems from belief, belief in the right of a person giving an order or instruction to be obeyed or followed. This means that 'authority' and 'compulsion' do not really belong together. A bully is not exercising authority when he compels a smaller and weaker person to do what he wants, but is forcing his will upon another person through the exercise of what may be called 'naked power.' Authority, on the other hand, involves the recognition by certain people that another person has the right to exercise power. This means that we can go a long way towards answering our question, 'Should we always obey those in authority?' by asking another, 'Have they the right to demand what they are asking?'

## Power exercised legitimately

The view that authority is power exercised legitimately can be illustrated by the attitude of the public at large to certain groups within it, such as the police, teachers, and government officials. Much of the prestige of the police, for example, depends upon the recognition by society that when a policeman is on duty he has the right to expect co-operation and obedience. A policeman is not obeyed simply because of the sanctions he may use against us if we disobey, but rather because we believe he has the right to expect us to obey him.

In recent years there have been some serious crises in authority. Demonstrators have refused to obey police, pupils have refused to conform to school rules, sections of the public have tried to ignore the authority of the state. Some, disturbed by this growing disrespect for 'the authorities' (as they sometimes call them), may then over-react by demanding that authority be imposed by means of stronger sanctions against those who disobey. So, for example, there has been a demand for British policemen to carry guns. In the sense in which I am using the word, however, authority cannot be imposed; it has to be accepted, believed in, recognised. Where disbelief in a person's right to exercise power is present, real authority is absent.

This view of authority finds support in the New Testament, for the Greek word *exousia*, usually translated 'authority', carries with it the idea of power being exercised legitimately. Jesus talks about having the right (*exousia*) to lay down his life and to take it again (John 10:18), and demonstrates that he has the right (*exousia*) to forgive sins by healing the paralytic (Matthew 9:6–8). Paul claimed the right (*exousia*) to marry and to expect financial support from the church he was serving (1 Corinthians 9:4) and clearly believed that God had authority over people just as a potter had authority (*exousia*) over his clay (Romans 9:21).

Against this brief New Testament background, we can begin to see how Christians ought to answer the question, 'Should we always obey those in authority?'

## The source of authority

First, it can be seen quite clearly that ultimate authority rests with God, for as Creator and Redeemer he is Sovereign Lord over all. We owe him complete obedience. But how can we know what God wants in order that we may obey him?

The answer is closely related to the Christian belief that Christianity is a revealed religion, which means, in short, that God has not left us to grope our way towards him but has taken the trouble to reveal himself and his will to us. God has revealed himself uniquely in the person of Jesus Christ, the Incarnate Word, and all that we need to know of God-revealed-in-Christ is contained in the Bible, the written Word. We know God's will by listening to Jesus: we hear Jesus by reading the Bible.

What this means in practical terms for everyday Christian living, and not least for an answer to our original question, is that the Bible is the norm, the yardstick against which our beliefs and practices have to be measured. So what does the Bible say about whether we should always obey those in authority?

The Bible makes it clear that where there is a direct conflict between the known will of God and some human demand, then God's will should be done. So, for example, Daniel was right to refuse the imperial edict forbidding him to pray to God (Daniel 6), and Peter and John were right to refuse the Jewish Sanhedrin's order to give up preaching about the resurrection (Acts 4:19). On both occasions, believers chose to obey God rather than men. It would not be difficult to find similar modern examples. But it must be remembered that the choice may be a costly one.

### National and family life

After allowing this overriding principle that obedience to God takes precedence over obedience to any human being or institution, the Bible sets out the general rule that Christians should obey those who legitimately exercise power over them. In the nation, for example, Christians are commanded to obey the government (Romans 13:1–6) in such practical matters as keeping the laws and paying taxes, for, says Paul, 'the authorities are in God's service.' In a democracy, Christians have the added incentive of knowing that they can help to create a more just (and therefore more Christian) society by the way they use their vote and exercise their influence.

Paul, like Moses before him, also had something to say about where authority lies in family life, for after making the general point, 'Be subject to one another out of reverence for Christ' (Ephesians 5:21), he went on to say, 'Wives, be subject to your husbands as to the Lord' (v. 22), 'Husbands, love your wives, as Christ also loved the church' (v. 25), and 'Children, obey your parents' (Ephesians 6:1).

The same writer proceeded to deal with relationships between 'slaves' and 'earthly masters,' and although under the influence of the gospel slavery was eventually abolished, the principles Paul set out in Ephesians 6:5–9 will repay study, and are capable of being applied to some extent to the relationship between employers and employees.

Should we always obey those in authority? The biblical answer seems clear. Yes, provided that what they demand is not in direct conflict with what God demands. But this does not mean that the Christian must not try to get the 'authorities' (national, managerial, paternal, or any others) to change their minds or modify their demands, if this should seem to be necessary in the interests of truth and justice.

**Maurice C. Burrell**

**Further reading**
*The Bible and the Crisis of Authority* J. R. W. Stott (Falcon)
*By What Authority?* William Barclay (SCM)

# 4
# Are pain and suffering direct results of evil?

The first need in tackling this question is to clarify what we mean by *evil*. Confusion here is common. I take the word to mean badness of a moral sort – badness which we recognise as good gone wrong, and which we feel ought not to exist at all. *Bad* is also used, of course, in non-moral ways, with such meanings as sub-standard (*eg*, a bad performance), unpleasant (*eg*, a bad taste), or unhappy in its results (*eg*, a bad move). But moral evil is a different thing from these.

When you boil it down, there are two kinds of things that we feel are morally bad. The first is the wrongdoing of moral agents, the badness of those who express vicious wills in vicious deeds. The second is pain and suffering that seems unproductive, meaningless, and a waste of good so far as the sufferer is concerned. Evil of both kinds is felt as a problem; if God is really good and really almighty, how can he allow either to exist? We shall see the answer to this question later.

## Pain has a purpose

To clear the ground, however, let it be said at once that not all pain is evil. Often pain is a needed warning, for which we should be thankful. When our hand hurts through inadvertent contact with a naked flame or boiling water, we are prompted to withdraw it at once – and a good thing too. If, like lepers, or those unhappy children who suffer from what doctors call congenital indifference to pain, we could not feel the hurt of our hand at such times, we should soon suffer fearful damage. So, too, it is a mercy when a pain in your head or your chest warns you that you are under too much strain, and need a rest.

Similarly, physical and mental suffering when bravely borne can produce nobility of character and a depth of creativeness that would not otherwise be there. Was Beethoven's deafness, the endless buzzing in his ears and the misery of isolation that it brought, an evil thing, when it produced the Eroica, the fifth and the ninth symphonies? Was Paul's thorn in the flesh an evil, when it led him into a deeper experience of grace (2 Corinthians 12:7–10)? Trouble has been called the chisel with which God sculpts our souls; it is no more morally evil than is the jarring of the nerve while the dentist drills your tooth.

### Sin and Satan

But, granted all that, sin and much seemingly unproductive suffering remain. Where do they come from? There is mystery here, but the following points sum up as much as Scripture tells us.

God is not the source of sin; he neither commits, nor wills, nor prompts it. 'God cannot be tempted with evil and he himself tempts no one' (James 1:13). God made rational creatures who were capable of loving him freely and by choice, and that meant that they could freely choose not to love him – which is what some angels and all our race have in fact done. How such disobedience is possible, while God is lord of his world (which Scripture says he is), we cannot conceive; that it is possible is, however, undeniable, for it has happened.

● If we ask how sin entered the cosmos, Scripture replies that Satan (the name means 'adversary') and his angels rebelled against the Creator before man was made (*cf* 2 Peter 2:4; Jude 6), so that when the first human beings appeared 'that ancient serpent, who is the Devil and Satan' (Revelation 20:2) was there to trip them up (Genesis 3). And 'the tempter' (1 Thessalonians 3:5), the 'ruler' and 'god' of this world (John 14:30; 2 Corinthians 4:4), still marauds with serpentine cunning and lion-like savagery, 'seeking someone to devour' (1 Peter 5:8). It is right to trace moral evil back to Satan as its patron, promoter, producer, director and instigatory cause.

● But if the question is, whence come the inclinations to evil which I find in myself, and yield to so often, the Bible says their source is my own heart. 'Let no one say when he is tempted, "I am tempted by God;" . . . each person is tempted when he is lured and enticed by his own desire. Then desire when it has conceived gives birth to sin . . .'

(James 1:13*ff*). Jesus endorses this. 'Out of the heart of man come evil thoughts, fornication, theft, murder, adultery, coveting, wickedness, deceit, licentiousness, envy, slander, pride, foolishness. All these evil things come from within ...' (Mark 7:21*ff*). My 'heart' in biblical usage is the core of my personal being, the centre and root of the real 'me:' and what these passages tell me is that, just as a cripple's twisted leg makes him walk lame, so the motivational twist of my fallen heart – anti-God, anti-others, self-absorbed – constantly induces wrong attitudes and actions. Nor can I excuse these because they are inevitable (though they are), but I must acknowledge them in every case as my own fault, for, in the ordinary everyday sense of the phrase, my heart is in them. My wrong-doing originates in me, in that twist of nature which we call original sin. G. K. Chesterton understood this. That was why, contributing to a newspaper correspondence on 'What's wrong with the world?' he simply wrote: 'Dear Sir, I am, Yours sincerely, G. K. C.'

● If, now, our enquiry moves on from human sin to human suffering, the following things may be said.

First, Scripture sees the whole cosmos as cursed and out of joint. This curse is part of God's just judgement on human sin (Genesis 3:17*ff*; Romans 3:19–23). The creation has been subjected to 'futility' (*ie*, non-achievement of its end, and failure to achieve any worthwhile end at all). We are not told in detail what this subjection involved, but it is natural to suppose that, just as physical death in the form in which we know it belongs to the curse (Genesis 3:3, 19; Romans 6:23), so death-dealers like cancer would not be as they are, were it not for the curse. The curse is one source, then, of pain and sickness, and for those who are not Christians there is no final remedy.

Second, Christians follow Jesus, who endured 'from sinners such hostility against himself' (Hebrews 12:3); and active human hostility against them, as against their Master, springs from the adverse reaction of sin-twisted nature to godliness in others – a reaction which is regularly destructive in intent. Here is a second source of suffering in this world.

Third, God is training all his children to enjoy a future life in which it is promised that tears and tribulation will be a thing of the past (Revelation 7:14–17; *cf* Hebrews 12:2). Whatever we find ourselves experiencing, therefore, of the curse on creation or hostility to the godly, should be thought of as part of the present discipline whereby God teaches us patience, courage, humility, faithfulness, and similar lessons, and as originating in his own plan for our sanctification (Hebrews 12:5–11).

Fourth, whatever perplexity may remain as to why this or that form of evil touches our lives, we should realise that what God in sovereign goodness did through Jesus's life, death and resurrection was to *handle* and *overcome* evil, with a view to eliminating it eventually from his world; and that what, in the same sovereign goodness, he wants us to learn is not primarily how to *explain* evil, but how to handle and overcome it for ourselves in Jesus's power. What matters is less that we should know its source than that we should know that God is now dealing with it to dispel it, and doing so in such a way that, in John Newton's words,

> Since all that I meet shall turn to my good,
>     The bitter is sweet, the medicine food!
> Though painful at present, 'twill cease before long,
>     And then, O how pleasant the conqueror's song!

**J. I. Packer**

**Further reading**
*The Problem of Pain* C. S. Lewis (Fontana)
*The Screwtape Letters* C. S. Lewis (Fontana)

# 5
# Are Christians hypocritical in preaching reconciliation when they themselves are so hopelessly divided?

We have to admit that the charge of division sticks. We may be able to say that in our particular locality things are not too bad: the churches get on well together, they meet regularly for an ecumenical week of prayer, they join in canvassing the locality for Christian Aid, they share an advertisement in the local paper every Easter and Christmas, and are friendly and co-operative towards each other.

But go to a city like Jerusalem, where scores of Christian denominations from all parts of the world feel they must have a stake, and you will see the scandal of our divisions. Centuries-old barriers of culture, language, theology and religious outlook separate churches which all claim to owe allegiance to Jesus Christ and continue to keep them apart – or at any rate to prevent them from understanding and harmonising with each other. The Christian observer, seeing such bewildering variety and sensing some of the tensions underlying the religious scene, wonders what Jew and Moslem make of it and he hides his face in shame.

## The given unity
It can be, and frequently is, argued that all true Christians *are* one,

that theirs is a given unity which needs needs no organisational effort to create. The unity produced by ecumenical 'planned marriages,' they say, is a false unity and runs counter to the true and spontaneous fellowship generated among men and women of like Christian faith.

This is altogether too naïve a position to hold. No one would deny that unity is a gift from God to his children and that there is a spiritual bond between all who serve and follow him; but the error comes in when I go on to imply that this unity is dependent on people thinking as *I* do and sharing *my* religious experience and *my* doctrinal presuppositions.

Quite clearly people will sense a greater degree of unity with those who are like-minded than with Christians who do not think as they do; but the fallacy of the argument is that it virtually defines the church by a concept of spiritual unity and unchurches those who fall outside its pre-set boundaries.

So we must quite honestly admit that as a church we do appear to be, and sometimes are, hopelessly divided. The explanation for this is to be found in all the vicissitudes of nineteen hundred years of church history. Doctrinal divisions have played their part, but so have national temperaments. The great divide between East and West in the early church owed much to the gulf between the Latin and Greek languages and the thought-forms to which they gave rise. How much confusion, for instance, has been caused to Christendom by the translation of *dikaiosis* (Greek) as *iustificatio* (Latin), the first meaning 'the act of declaring innocent' and the second suggesting a process of 'being made righteous.' Such confusion lies at the root of Catholic-Protestant division over justification by faith. In other cases a faulty understanding of the doctrine of the church has encouraged Protestant separatism and pseudo-perfectionism.

## Drawing closer together

Against all this, however, must be set the great improvements that have taken place in inter-church relationships during the twentieth century. Generations of in-built prejudice and insularity are fast disappearing and making way for brotherliness and co-operation. Inevitably they take a long time to disappear and there are cases where they can only be removed by a skilfully waged campaign for mutual understanding. Some things just will not happen if you adopt a policy of 'leaving it to the Spirit.'

But for all our notable failures, massive progress has been made and we are right to draw attention to it and to show that we are not nearly so divided as some of our critics would like to believe. Where unity schemes have failed, the reason has been due not to any lack of desire for closer co-operation but to the imperfections of the means whereby it is to be achieved, as in the abortive Anglican-Methodist scheme, or to secondary issues of a legal and organisational, rather than doctrinal, nature.

## The ministry of reconciliation

If the churches experience such difficulty in coming to the place of reconciliation among themselves, how can they with a clear conscience continue to preach a gospel of reconciliation? This is a perfectly fair question. Three points need to be made in reply.

● The church will always share the failings of the people to whom it preaches. Evangelism consists of fallen men speaking the good news to fallen men, or, as someone has put it, 'one beggar telling another beggar where bread is to be found.' The church cannot wait to be perfect before proclaiming her message. We preach the gospel not from a moral eminence but out of sympathy. Of course our voice will be heeded much more when we speak from holiness than when we are compromised by worldliness, but whatever our imperfections we must not remain silent. It would be an even greater hypocrisy to have the gospel of salvation and to keep it to ourselves.

● The charge of hypocrisy can be levelled against the church only if it preaches reconciliation and *at the same time* fails to set about the task of being reconciled with fellow-Christians within the church. Our Lord's teaching in Matthew 5:23*f* is the standard by which the church must live. Anything which conflicts with our living out the gospel of the love of God must be subjected to scrutiny if we are to have any hope of convincing the world that we are being consistent. Failure to do so cannot fail to nullify our Christian effectiveness.

● A united church does not mean a monochrome church, where traditions are forgotten and where everyone pretends to believe and to behave in the same way. As long as the church is peopled by human beings there will be diversity and variety. This is wholly good and scripturally right. Remember Paul's teaching about the different parts of the Body of Christ. The aim of the reconciling church in its ecumenical movement should be not uniformity but unity-in-diversity. There is no hypocrisy in wanting that.

**J. B. Taylor**

# 6

# Have we any right to persuade people of other religions to become Christians?

Whatever answer we think is right, the first thing to be clear about is our own attitude towards people of other faiths. This is important whether we meet them in this country or overseas.

## Respect for other religions

A right attitude begins by our recognising that they have a faith in their religion as strong or as weak as our own. They live by what they believe, or fail to do so, just as we do. Next, it is important to realise that, as far as this country is concerned, they are a minority group. As such, they feel themselves threatened. This makes them stick very closely together, and makes them very suspicious of any approach by Christians.

This attitude of theirs is wholly understandable and deserves our sympathy. Very few of them want to be assimilated to our way of life. They value their traditional culture. And in the culture of the Muslim or the Hindu or the Sikh or the Buddhist, religion enters into every part of life. For a Sikh, for instance, the wearing of a turban is part of his culture and his religion, something which our bureaucrats do not understand. With us, the wearing of a bowler hat or a cloth cap has nothing to do with our religion. For a Sikh, what he wears on his head really does matter.

Again, marriage traditions in the Hindu community and among Muslims are very different from ours. The freedom between the sexes which we enjoy, they view with great misgivings. Women's Lib is not a movement they either approve of or understand. That does not mean that they are stupid.

### How to treat 'strangers'

Our most important task at all times is to understand and respect the convictions of these 'strangers' who are our fellow-citizens. In the Bible there is quite a lot about the way to treat strangers. Exodus 2:21, Leviticus 19:33–34, Deuteronomy 10:18–19 are just three out of many references which show the ideal set before the people of Israel. They did not live up to it always, any more than we do. But we, as Christians, cannot have lower ideals. Matthew 25:35–43 has something very important to say about strangers. Hebrews 13:2 actually tells us to entertain them.

If we go abroad, and live in a country where we are aliens, and are often only a tiny handful of strangers in a Muslim, Hindu, or Buddhist culture, we soon realise the importance of these biblical guide-lines. When we ourselves are outsiders, the advice of Deuteronomy 10:19, 'Love the stranger' sounds good! And it applies the other way round.

We will never be able to think straight about the religious faith of other men until we get our attitude to them right. Only then can we begin to look for an answer to our question.

### Persuasion

What do we really mean by persuading people of other religions to become Christians? What kind of Christians do we want them to become? Are we sure that we know? Roman Catholics, Methodists, Presbyterians, Anglicans – all these are Christians, but the ways in which they express their faith and organise their common life are, in some respects, very different. Are we quite sure that any one of them is so absolutely right that we can ask the man or woman of another religion to choose, and be quite sure he will make the choice we think is the right one?

Obviously our question raises a lot of other questions.

But that is not the end of the matter. We live in a world full of suffering and sorrow, a world in which there is so much evil, a world in which death can be very sudden, in which dying can take such very unpleasant forms. Now, if we ourselves know someone who can help men and women to cope with this kind of world, who can give them hope and courage and joy, surely we ought at least to try to effect an introduction.

Persuading is always in danger of being a form of pressure. But simply to tell of our own experience of Jesus Christ as a Saviour who can meet all our needs, is quite different. We report what we know, we encourage our stranger-friend to read, perhaps, St Mark's Gospel, or one of the others. And we leave Jesus to make his own impact. Of course, we will pray for this stranger-friend of ours. We will also pray that our own lives may show what Jesus has done for us. But the other man, the other woman, is left free to say 'Yes' or 'No.'

This is the real Christian duty, whether we do it in our own street, or in India or Uganda or anywhere else. To know Jesus and what he has done for us, and is doing for us, and not to share the good news with others is just selfishness.

**M. A. C. Warren**

**Further reading**
*The World's Religions* ed Norman Anderson (IVP)

# 7
# What has Christianity to say about race relations and the colour problem?

'Race is an explosive subject! Almost any group of people can get involved in an animated debate on race – principles, prejudices, denunciations and passionate concern flying in all directions.' So David Bronnert begins his Falcon booklet *Race – the Challenge to Christians*. How right he is! When it was suggested in a newspaper that we must accept that ours is now a society permanently characterised by a multiplicity of creeds, racial origins, and ethnic identities, there were some bitter reactions in reply. One correspondent asked if the writer had any idea of the hate and tension building up among many white people in Britain. On the other side, a publication such as *Race Today* gives expression to the anger and bitterness of many in the black community.

Race and colour are not just problems for Britain. They are issues of world-wide significance. Through our newspapers and on our television screens we see evidence of racial conflict, we know of the evils that result from apartheid in South Africa, and we wonder if an all-out racial war will develop in the southern part of the African continent. Here is a great world question about which Christians need to do some pretty fast and thorough thinking. What is required of us by the Gospel?

**Bible teaching**
First, we need to understand correctly the teaching of Scriptures, and

not be misled by those who wrest its teaching to justify attitudes of racial superiority or policies of separate development. For instance, the curse of Noah (Genesis 9:25) has been used by the Dutch Reformed Church in South Africa to justify the perpetual subjection of black to white, whereas its application is clearly to the Canaanites who were of the same Semitic stock as the Hebrews. And some white people (who would be the first to take pride in the expansion of our stock and culture across the world) use St Paul's words at Athens (Acts 17:26) to justify keeping coloured people in their own countries and out of ours, whereas the whole drift of St Paul's sermon is 'the complete antithesis of an exclusive, nationalistic, racist spirit' (Bronnert).

When we look at the Bible teaching as a whole, we see that it is set in a universal context. All men, it proclaims, are made in the image of God. All are sinners. Christ died for all men. Christians of all races are one in Christ. God's eternal purpose is to gather together in one all things in Christ. True, many Old Testament passages do suggest a narrow Jewish particularism *vis-a-vis* neighbouring peoples, but the story does not end there. As we follow its sweep we see that the prophets repeatedly condemned a nationalism that forgets justice and mercy to the poor and the stranger within the gates and called God's people to be a light to the nations, that his salvation may reach to the end of the earth (Isaiah 49:6). The New Testament rejoices in the breaking down by Christ of the middle wall of partition between Jew and Gentile, and it closes with St John the seer's splendid vision of the City of God, by whose light the nations shall walk and into which their glory and splendour shall be brought (Revelations 21:24–26).

### British history

Next we need to look back at our history over the last 200 years. British people have emigrated in their thousands to new lands (often fighting the original inhabitants). Before Wilberforce, Britain was deeply involved in the slave trade to North America and the Caribbean.

Throughout the remainder of the 19th century she painted large parts of the map of the world red. The Empire supplied us with cheap raw materials for manufacture, and the finished products were then exported to the world at great profit. 'We showed that wealth and power were to be found in Britain. We (also) fostered the idea of

Britain as the motherland of the people we colonised' (*And Who is my Neighbour?* British Council of Churches Community and Race Relations Unit pamphlet).

Furthermore, the pamphlet continues, 'in the period of labour shortage after the war, we actively encouraged people from these countries to come to Britain to do the less desirable jobs (even going so far as to set up recruiting centres in some places).' We didn't ask them to come here? In fact, that is just what we did. And many are doing jobs that other people will not do. For instance, our transport and health service would collapse without the help of the New Commonwealth immigrants.

What about the East African Asians? Well, when Kenya, Uganda and Tanzania became independent, we gave these people the opportunity of retaining British nationality if they did not wish to apply for citizenship in the new nations. We are in honour bound to accept those expelled from East Africa who hold British passports and have nowhere else to go.

On any realistic understanding of the situation then, we must accept that from now on, there will be a coloured population of some two million or so within the fifty million inhabitants of Great Britain.

What should our attitude be to them? In the light of the basic teaching of the Bible, we can have no doubt about the answer. We cannot treat as second-class citizens those who, whatever their colour, share the humanity which the Son of God took upon him in the Incarnation and which he has redeemed by dying for us.

### Christian responsibility

In consequence, Christian citizens in this country have great responsibilities laid upon them. First, we must get to know the facts about legislation and other official action designed both to restrict immigration and to ensure justice for all. We should learn too about the various and conflicting pressures of public opinion which lie behind these actions. We need to know also the truth in contrast to the parrot cries about immigrants coming to live off our social security system and the calls that they should be encouraged, if not pressurised, to return home. For example it is a fact that many have no homes outside Britain, whilst many of the younger generation have been born and brought up here and know no other country. We must be ready to speak up and be counted when white communities, which pride themselves on having no race problem, show themselves acutely racist. That may well require of us individually some self-examination first!

Then we have positive responsibilities towards New Britons. We should behave towards them with the same courtesy and good neighbourliness that we show people of our own race. We should take time and trouble to build bridges of understanding. We could visit a West Indian Pentecostal Church or a Sikh temple or invite overseas students and others to our homes. We should keep watch on policies in our area in regard to job opportunities, housing, education etc. and be ready to write to the local paper, supporting a local community project etc. In these days of pressure groups, Christians in a city or town should stand together and when necessary challenge their MP or the local councillors when injustices occur.

What part should the Church at the national or local level be playing? It *should* be a shining example of a Christian fellowship which rises above the restricted outlook of a particular section of society (most often white and middle-class). In Christ's name, it should work for a nation in which all receive just and equal treatment and all can bring their particular contribution to the enrichment of the whole community. For instance, are we ready to make buildings available for Christians whose forms of worship may suggest 'pentecostal pandemonium' rather than our own more sedate and traditional ways? Are we prepared to allow our premises to be used for the social gatherings of people of other faiths – and, in so far as conscience allows, for religious purposes? Would we consider selling a redundant church building to such a group? Or are we 'just a replica of society – an "in" group, protecting our special privileges, our property and position, against threats from those outside?' (Gwen Cashmore, USPC, Bray Lecture 1975).

What about evangelism? Is that not our first and major responsibility? Perhaps we have something to learn here from General Booth. As he viewed the vast areas of poverty of our great cities with their disinherited and unchurched masses, he set out his order in the slogan – soup, soap and salvation. It is only as our congregations are seen to be servants of the community, ready to minister to the local situation in any way they can, that the message they proclaim has any possibility of being heard. Only if, like our Master, we are ready not to be ministered to but to minister, and to identify at whatever cost with those who too often get a raw deal in our society, shall we commend the saving Gospel of Jesus Christ and open the way to response.

**Kenneth Sansbury**

**Further reading**

*Ethnic Minorities in Society*: a reference guide (British Council of Churches)

*World Religions in Britain*: three study pamphlets, Mariyan Mahmoud-Harris (BCC)

*The New Black Presence*: A Christian Scrutiny (BCC)

*Race Relations*: study notes on the Bible, David Bronnert (BCC)

*Race – the Challenge to Christians* David Bronnert (Falcon)

Further information on this subject is obtainable from the Community and Race Relations Unit of the British Council of Churches (10 Eaton Gate, London, SW1W 9BT) and from the Evangelical Race Relations Group (269 Rotton Park Road, Birmingham, B16 OLD).

# 8

# Can a Christian subscribe to the view that a woman is a second class citizen?

Mary and Jane met outside church one Sunday morning. Jane was evidently feeling very frustrated after she had spent a long time with the vicar the previous evening in discussion about her future career.

'I told him,' she said, 'that I wanted to serve the Church as he does, as a minister of religion, and he told me that was quite impossible because only men can serve God in that way. He suggested that I'd make a good nurse or missionary, and be much more use to God doing what women were intended to do – act as helpmeets to men – at any rate until they got married and became mothers. He implied that I wanted to be a man and not a proper woman if I thought I could do a "man's job," and he also made me feel I wasn't worth a good education. He made me feel second class!'

'Well, you're not!' replied her friend. 'You know that perfectly well. You may be different from a man but you're certainly equal to him in the sight of God and as deeply loved by God as anyone else. You seem so upset about it though. Are you sure you've got hold of the right end of the stick?'

'Yes, I am,' Jane said. 'He told me to go and look at Genesis (Genesis 2–3) and at what St Paul had said in his letter to the Corinthians about Christ being the head of the man and man the head of woman; and about women having to keep silence in church and ask their questions of their husbands at home' (1 Corinthians 11:3 *ff*). 'And Timothy,' she added, 'and all that bit about women "listening quietly and with due submission" and not being teachers or domineering over men, but being saved by childbirth (1 Timothy 2). Well, what if I don't get married? Am I supposed to make quite sure that I never get a job where I might have to teach a man or tell him what to do? Ugh – I'm beginning to hate men,' she added, 'they're so superior and sure of themselves and they can always quote the Bible at you and win the argument that way. It makes you want to throw the Bible at them sometimes.'

Mary tossed her head and laughed. 'Goodness,' she said, 'he has touched you on the raw. Perhaps you don't feel so confident about God wanting you to be a minister as you were when we talked about it last Sunday.'

'Well, I'm not,' said Jane. 'I thought he'd laugh a bit, but not that he'd quote all that out-dated stuff from the Bible at me. And yet, when he did I found that I half believed it all myself and that's what makes me feel so horribly inferior and second class inside myself, and makes it seem crazy to want to be a woman minister.'

'Don't be so sure about the Bible being out-dated,' Mary told her. 'Of course, you can make the Bible support almost any point of view if you are determined to bend the words to your own ideas. But the Bible *does* reveal the mind of God to us: only to get the whole picture straight the vicar ought to have told you to read Genesis 1 as well as Genesis 2–3 and suggested that you look at the words St Paul wrote to the Corinthians a little earlier in his letter to them. At the beginning of chapter 7 you'll find some of the most beautiful and profound words he ever wrote about the partnership of husband and wife in marriage. A little further on there's an even more important bit about a baptised wife being able to save her heathen husband because "the heathen husband now belongs to God through his Christian wife" (1 Corinthians 7:14). No second class for women there, nor in his attitude to men and women in Christ in Galatians 3:28 where he says "you are all one person in Christ Jesus." But what really surprises me is that neither you nor the vicar seem to have talked about Jesus's attitude to women and men in the Gospels.'

'What do you mean?' Jane asked her friend. She was really listening now.

'Well,' Mary said, 'just look at how Jesus broke all the rules for good Jewish men of his day. He spoke to a woman of Samaria in public (John 4:1–30). He allowed an unclean woman to touch him and apparently never troubled with the proper ritual purification before going on to heal Jairus's daughter. (Luke 8:43 ƒ). He allowed a woman to anoint him with oil for his death (Mark 14.1–9). And after his death Jesus appeared first of all to a woman, at a time in Jewish history when women were treated as minors, like children, and weren't allowed to be witnesses in lawcourts. Jesus certainly never treated women as second class citizens and his disciples must have picked up his attitudes too. Otherwise why would they have broken with all the Jewish norms of behaviour and admitted women to baptism? I think that fact is tremendously important, and the proof of it is in Acts where we are told that Mary and a group of women were present at Pentecost. Look at Acts 1:14 and at chapter 2. There never has been any second class citizenship in Christianity and women have suffered as martyrs for Christ and have been recognised as his saints.'

'I wish it felt that way,' said Jane.

'I think we have to face the fact that the Church has treated women as second class citizens far too often, and that is a shame to the Church,' said Mary. 'Even in our time few churches make the best use of women's gifts. I think it's quite possible that men may have misunderstood Jesus's mind about women and it's only now that many churches are beginning to accept women as full people. It may not help you much, but, you know there are churches which do have ordained women ministers, like the Methodists, Baptists and United Reformed Churches. Give the vicar a bit of time and he may come round to it yet.'

'What will I do, meantime?' Jane said.

'Show that you're a first class citizen of the Kingdom of God, whatever people may say,' said Mary. 'Pray and study and serve God; yes, and argue a little with the vicar from time to time, because otherwise he'll just prove his point that women can't think as well as men, nor serve Christ in the same way. You may never marry yourself, but whatever you do, don't despise your own womanhood, nor motherhood if it ever comes your way.'

'Thanks, Mary,' said Jane. 'I feel a bit more confident now that you've helped me to see things a bit straighter.'

**Una Kroll**

**Further reading**
*More Than a Spare Rib* Una Kroll

# 9
# Why isn't the church's voice heard more in the political arena?

The answer to the question depends entirely on what you think of politics.

'Politics,' says Ambrose Bierce in his *Devil's Dictionary*, 'is a strife of interests masquerading as a contest of principles; the conduct of public affairs for private advantage.' But that is the devil's definition. In its original sense, politics means simply the 'science of government' – and as government inevitably has profound consequences for those who are governed, it is unthinkable that the Church's voice should not be heard in the political arena.

The prophets of the Old Testament certainly made their voices heard. They talked vociferously about the vices of the king and the greed of the landowners, about inflation and international treaties, about injustice and luxury. Amos, for example came to be regarded as a political agitator and a menace to the establishment. Jeremiah was imprisoned because he spoke against the war. The prophets took up their unenviable task at the command of God because they were concerned about the effects of government upon the common man. It was their way of loving God and loving their neighbour.

Given the fact then that the voice of the Church ought to be heard in the political arena, how is it to be heard? Bishops speak in the House of Lords, clergy write to Members of Parliament, Christian academics contribute to the correspondence columns of *The Times*, the General Synod of the Church of England forwards resolutions to the Prime Minister. But this scarcely adds up to 'the voice of the Church.' Well, then what can be done? I suggest three possibilities.

## The layman's witness

First, individual Christians who might be listening for a call to the ordained ministry or to the mission field, to the social services or to medicine, should be alert to the possibility of another calling, *ie* the science of government, or politics. The prophets were for the large part laymen called of God to influence the decisions which their rulers were making and to summon the nation to the bar of God's judgement. They were not spectacularly successful at the time, but their utterances live on as a constant challenge to rulers and politicians and government officials.

The church's voice, if it is to be heard at all, will be heard from within the political arena rather than from outside it. The spectator may see more of the game but he has scarcely any capacity for influencing the result. The committed Marxist is often to be found in the places of maximum power and influence. He has no need to raise his voice in public. He may be just an under-secretary or the head of a department or a newspaper's correspondent for political affairs or the convenor of his union branch. Good luck to him – he deserves his success. But it would be a pity if the Christian case, which is often a thoroughly practical and persuasive one, should go by default for lack of anyone to sustain it.

## The local community

Second, the local church should take the science of government seriously and accept its responsibility at local and national level. There are many practising Christians in both Houses of Parliament, many more in local government and in union management. They need to feel a ground-swell of support from the church; they need more help than they commonly get from the congregations to which they belong.

I seldom hear prayers in church for the local officials by name. What about the Member of Parliament who may be involved in a crucial debate the following week, or for the local councillor who has to chair an important meeting on housing on Monday evening, or for the shop steward at the local works as he struggles with some bitter industrial dispute? They need to be remembered personally. There are some parishes big enough and flourishing enough to constitute themselves into 'support groups' who would make it their business, not only to pray, but to know and to act.

## Church and nation

Then the Church as a whole should attend with greater seriousness to public affairs. If the reaction to the Archbishops' Initiative in October 1975 is anything to go by, there are more people than we sometimes imagine who are calling to the Church to do just that. For the past three or four hundred years, for reasons good and for reasons bad, the Church in the United Kingdom has been steadily withdrawing from public life. The time has come to arrest the drift. The time has come to try to articulate in political terms the kind of Christian aspirations to which many millions of our countrymen still give silent assent.

Too often we simply react to pressures from outside or protest at decisions already made. We trail rather limply in the wake of enthusiastic but unbalanced minority movements or climb on to bandwagons at just the point where they are grinding to a halt. This is no way for the Church of God to handle its responsibilities to the nation. We enjoy marvellous resources of knowledge, expertise and devotion in the church, but no apparent means of mobilising them in the interests of a clear and practical approach to the great issues which trouble us all. The leaders of the churches have some responsibility for being also leaders of the nation.

'Ah,' you will say, 'the Church can never agree about anything. How can we achieve a Christian consensus in politics?' No consensus is necessary. It is only necessary that Christians should have been exposed to the realities of the political situation and are thus able to react to them in the light of their own conscience, aided, I trust, by the mind of the Church as it has been exhibited down the centuries. We are not looking for a Christian political party, subject to the whips, voting one way, huddling together, but for Christians in every party of every persuasion who will act and try to cause others to act against the background of God's prevailing will for mankind. We need men and women who are as devoted to God's kingdom as they are to the United Kingdom.

'Render to Caesar the things that are Caesar's, and to God the things that are God's,' Jesus said. We have not begun to penetrate to the meaning of those enigmatic words, but at least they suggest that there are duties to Caesar and there are duties to God. The duties to

Caesar are as arduous as the duties to God and not seldom prove to be singularly frustrating.

Politics is the art of the possible, and compromise is inseparable from it. Solid results depend on the willingness to accept certain conventions and certain inescapable conditions. The author of Ecclesiastes tells how 'there was a little city and a few men within it; and there came a great king against it and besieged it, and built great bulwarks against it. Now there was found in it a poor wise man, and he by his wisdom delivered the city. Yet no man remembered that same poor man' (Ecclesiastes 9:14–15). No matter – he did deliver the city.

The Christian in public affairs may not make a name for himself. He may get precious little thanks. But by the gift of divine wisdom he may be enabled to deliver the city.

**Stuart Ebor**

# 10

# Should Christianity be anti-communist?

'A Christian *must* be a Communist. All men are equal in the sight of God. Jesus was the first Communist.'

Most of us have heard such statements as these, the speaker often apparently feeling that the opinion he is expressing is self-evident and obvious. We might thus be provoked into over-reacting in either of two ways, either in agreeing unintentionally to limiting the Gospel to a thing of this world only, or on the other hand denying that it has any social relevance whatever.

As Christians we need to respond wisely and bravely as we meet Communism as a world force, as it features in our national life, and as we meet individual Communists or Marxists in our daily lives. Also it is good to have some understanding of the issues confronting our fellow Christians in Communist countries, so that we can help them more effectively, both in prayer and in practical ways wherever possible.

To gain a right viewpoint on this matter, it will help if we begin with a proper idea of the equality of all men before God. This includes things much greater than giving to all men according to their material needs; it embraces the fact that before the infinite majesty of God all men, even the greatest, are as nothing, and yet all men are created in the image of God, significant, and that Christ died for all.

These several ideas, which have exercised the minds of great theologians, should powerfully affect us. One thing they will do is to make us aware of how wrong it is to mistreat another man.

## Communism and religion

Secondly, we must remember that atheism is a central feature of Communism as conceived by Marx and his followers. And as the Communist looks at the world he sees conflict and oppression underlying it, the classes of owners and workers irreconcilably set against each other until things reach a point where the working class overthrow their overlords, so gaining control for themselves of the means of production and the goods *they* produce. The success of this revolution, although it will almost certainly be violent, is the door of hope for mankind.

The Communist sees two functions that religion play. On the one hand it is what Marx called 'the opium of the people, the sigh of the oppressed.' Influenced by the grinding poverty of working people in 19th century England, he concluded that in such a condition religion, although only an illusion fed by despair, provided for such people some comfort, some hope of happiness in another world, but kept them from looking objectively at this world with its social evils and injustices. On the other hand the ruling classes could use religion to their own advantage by pointing out that the gods (or God) command obedience. Incidentally, Marx and Lenin seemed to see no important difference between the crude tyranny exercised by a witch-doctor in a primitive tribe and the Christian view of authority, which commands obedience but also reminds all men, and particularly rulers, that they are responsible to God and that authority is only rightly used when used as God directs, *ie* to further justice, including social justice. This Christian view is a great incentive to men to act maturely in society.

## Revolution

Evidently the Christian must conclude that the Communist outlook contains half-truths. It is true that all is far from right in this world which has rebelled against God – and class conflict and oppression are part of this trouble, and arguably might even justify revolt in extreme circumstances. However, Scripture maintains that God thinks it best that there be governments, which inevitably will consist of at best imperfect and often corrupt men, who yet have the office of ruling in order to restrain evil and promote the welfare of the population as a whole (Romans 13:1–7).

The suggestion that revolution can lead to a final solution of all man's problems is dangerous because it promotes an optimism for revolution at the expense of attempts at non-violent change. It is very difficult to know ahead of time whether the human suffering caused by a revolution whether successful or not and its aftermath will not be greater than that caused by the injustices it seeks to be remedying. Furthermore, the suggestion is false: it neglects man's sinful nature, which is such that the new society itself will still have human failings, while at the same time it promotes ideas of self-righteousness in the minds of revolutionaries, so that even if they are very noble at the beginning they may be hardened from taking rebuke or advice and their rule become oppressive in its turn, even against those sections of society it claims to be helping.

## The Christian attitude

From this it follows that Christianity may rightly be called anti-Communist in the sense that it exposes Communism's goals as being unattainable on the latter's own conditions, and the attempt to attain them in that way as fraught with hazard. Furthermore, we should not hold back from calling deceitful claims to social achievements which Communist governments say they have made before these have been attained; and we should support and initiate efforts for the gaining of greater religious and other freedom in Communist lands. To do this effectively we shall need to be informed of what the situation really is.

There are two dangers that we must beware of here. We have to strike a correct balance between our relationship to God and our dealings with other people. It can happen that as we begin to see quite rightly that the righteousness in which the kingdom of God consists goes beyond a private holiness into helping others, we become so caught up as to forget that our personal 'walk' with God is fundamental. 'A good tree cannot bring forth evil fruit. . . .' Secondly by getting into a bad habit of believing without checking *every* disparaging report that concerns Communism we drift towards an extremist position on the other side. This danger is especially important for anyone to avoid who is seeking to serve his fellow Christians living in Communist countries.

Opposition to Communist ideology and methods does not imply that Christians oppose freedom of speech for Communists. We should not and do not do so, nor should we allow the suggestion or insinuation to go unchallenged. Rather we welcome open discussion so that we may persuade men about our faith, which we present in humility, perhaps in weakness, believing it to be the power of God to salvation.

**Richard Ablitt**

**Further reading**
*The Sky is Red* Geoffrey Bull (Hodders)
*Three Generations of Suffering* G. Vins (Hodders)
*A Christian Manifesto to a Socialist Society* I. Ton (IVP)
*The Communist Manifesto* (Penguin)

# 11

# What is the Church's teaching about exorcism?

The practice of expelling evil spirits is not a peculiarly Christian activity. It has been attempted for centuries by Jews, Hindus and others. Biblically we must see it against the background of ceaseless cosmic conflict and supremely in the light of the authority of Christ, whose arrival and ministry on earth spelt out the end of demonic domination. But what are demons? Little is said about them in the Old Testament, and relatively little in the New Testament book of Acts, or in the Epistles. It is only when we come to the Gospels that we find numerous references to them – their manifestation evidently featuring as a violent reaction of the powers of evil against the person and work of Jesus. In the Gospels there is no doubt that evil spirits are seen as spiritual beings totally opposed to the kingdom of God, and that they recognise Christ as their superior and as the source of their ultimate destruction (Matthew 8:29).

## Demonic activity

It is also important to see that demonic activity is not simply a first century way of describing mental illness, for the Gospel writers themselves distinguish between such categories as the sick, the diseased, the demoniacs, epileptics and paralytics (Matthew 4:24). While the fact of evil spirits has long been recognised in pagan cultures, it is only in recent years that the supposedly Christian cultures of the West have begun to acknowledge their presence – and money-spinning films such as *Rosemary's Baby* and *The Exorcist* have given an added boost to such interest. It seems that while a society has the benefit of Christian values and a strong church, these act as a buffer against occult activity; but once they are rejected, the door is opened for a more direct interference by satanic influences. In the same way the Christian is safe from the influence of magic spells and demon oppression, provided there is care taken to avoid all involvement in occult activity.

Two girls were attending a party. Suddenly a ouija board was produced, and everyone was invited to take a turn at asking questions of 'the spirit,' with answers purportedly given through an inverted tumbler as it moved about the board. 'I'm not staying,' announced one of the two girls. 'Come on, Jean.' And she literally dragged her friend by the arm, and took her into another room. Only the Sunday before she had heard a sermon in church about the dangers of involvement in occult activities – even if only in fun – and she was on her guard.

It is not that attendance at a ouija board session *necessarily* results in bondage of one form or another. Plenty of people have 'dabbled' a little and have emerged unscathed. But even the mildest dabbling means that the person involved is stepping out from under the protective umbrella that may so far have been afforded him.

## Occult involvement

Occult involvement is on two levels, basically. There is the school playground experiment level, which may result in one or more of the participants receiving a thorough fright. Such problems encountered are comparatively mild, and can be resolved through the prayer and counselling of an experienced Christian leader. However, there is the more serious level resulting, usually, from persistent dabbling, or from a deliberate desire to make contact with the unseen world. I have a few points that I think are worth making here – observations based on the findings of more than a few ministers and leaders who have been required to assist in cases of occult bondage.

First, the afflicted person cannot be freed unless there is a genuine willingness to renounce such occult involvement as has taken place. There is no point at all in any prayer of release taking place unless there is a degree of co-operation on the part of the one needing help. Indeed the Christian counsellor may well come under attack himself if a premature prayer of liberation is attempted.

Secondly, such counselling should not be attempted alone – and never by inexperienced workers. This principle surely is what lies behind the tightening-up policy regarding exorcism on the part of many church leaders in recent times. There have been too many casualties, resulting from the efforts of people who all too often have developed a taste for exorcism. Such people are very dangerous indeed. If a counsellor cannot tell the difference between occult bondage and mental illness, for example, the damage done may be immense. Some psychiatric training is valuable in this field of counselling.

Thirdly, it follows that the matter of diagnosis is vital. Let us suppose that the counsellor is faced with what appears to be a case of genuine demon possession and such cases are not as common as is supposed in some circles. *He must never speak of his suspicions to the person concerned.* For after all, his diagnosis may be faulty – in which case he will have done terrible harm. The procedure should rather be steady and unhurried. If there is deep occult involvement, then the regular and prayerful support of a group of Christian friends is highly desirable. A step-by-step approach is infinitely to be preferred to the impatience that seeks an early and quick liberation.

Fourthly, the relationship between the counsellor and Christ himself is of supreme importance. Releasing someone from occult bondage is not a matter of using certain formulae, the right words and phrases, however correct and scriptural. Indeed, once start to *use* the name of Christ in this way and you are teetering on the edge of mediumism and white magic, which draws its power ultimately from below. The counsellor can do no more than place himself prayerfully at the disposal of Christ, and under his protection and authority. He will be aware of the power of Christ's blood shed at Calvary, by which victory over the demonic world is assured (Colossians 2:15; Revelation 12:11). But he will never try to 'force a result,' or use the Lord's name as a charm or magic formula. Mentally he will never be sitting in the driving seat himself. There are plenty of modern counterparts to the incident recorded in Acts 19:13–20, in which a group of itinerant exorcists had to learn the lesson that Christ's name is not to be trafficked with.

Thus when it comes to genuine Christian ministry and exorcism, the important factor is not the 'act' of exorcism. Neither does it involve any amount of laying-on-of-hands – an act that in any case is to be discouraged in dealing with the occult; our Lord does not appear to have used it – nor a use of crosses, holy water, nor even the *use* of the Holy Communion. The all-important factor is that of truth, and the authority of Christ himself. Only this can bring about the lasting banishment of the fear, illusions and revulsion to spiritual things resulting from occult involvement.

A mature Christian leader with a fund of experience and with the backing of the Church may well be called by God into this field. But it is certainly not for the inexperienced.

**Richard Bewes**

**Further reading**
*The Occult* David Gillett (Falcon)
*Christianity and the Occult* J. Stafford Wright (Scripture Union)
*Demonology Past and Present* Kurt Koch (Kregel Publications)
*Christian Counselling and Occultism* Kurt Koch (Evangelization Publications)

## 12

# Are experiments in genetics against God's will?

The idea that the genetical composition of any organism – plant, animal or man – is somehow sacrosanct is based on both a theological and a scientific fallacy.

**Theological considerations**
In Genesis 1 and 2 we read that God made all living creatures 'according to their kind,' that they were good, and that Adam gave names to every 'kind' of animal. We are nowhere told in the Bible that the biological state of affairs existing at the time Adam was in Eden was to be unchanged for the rest of the world's history. There are many recorded examples of both extinction and intra-specific genetical change which have nothing to do with human avarice and sin (*ie* the effects of the Fall), but which have substantially changed the fauna and flora of many lands in the past few centuries.

More important, it is naïve and incorrect to regard the 'image of God' which distinguishes man from the animals (Genesis 1:27, 2:7) as related in any way to his *biological* characteristics (*sensu stricto*). Only if God is literally a paternal monarch do we have to regard our head, hands, digestive system, and so on as made on the same pattern as his. In fact the Bible is at pains to emphasise God's transcendental divinity (*eg* Psalm 121:4, John 4:24), and to distinguish this from the times he took human form (in various Old Testament theophanies, and particularly as Jesus, son of Mary). The New Testament writers repeatedly point out the need for individual repentance and faith, and the comparative irrelevance for salvation of heredity (*eg* John 1:13, 1 Peter 1:22, 23). Even the comparison by Paul of the effects of Adam's and Christ's deaths (Romans 5:12–17) does not necessarily involve the genetical ancestry of Adam to the whole of the human race, since it is spiritual and not physical consequences that are the concern of Paul. In fact, Adam lived many years after his spiritual death in Eden (*cf* Romans 9:8). Our genes and chromosomes are a necessary part of our nature as body-souls, but are spiritually no more (or less) significant than our feet, eyes, ears or 'unpresentable parts' (1 Corinthians 12:14–26).

## Scientific

Early work in radiation genetics apparently showed that the genetical material was almost mystically stable, able to be changed (or *mutated*) only by high energy radiation. The discovery of chemicals which produced mutations and the realisation that many cells are capable of repairing a considerable amount of genetical damage (the early mutation experiments were largely carried out on mature sperm which are metabolically almost inert), has led to a fuller interpretation: that the DNA and protein which make up the genes and chromosomes are just as reactive as similar molecules with different functions. The present understanding of the genetical content of an individual or group is that it undergoes continual change, but that most of the altered forms are eliminated by repair, cell death, or reduced fertility. Ageing and many cancers are the result of the accumulation of genetical changes during life.

There are some people who regard all experiment or 'interference' with 'natural' processes as wrong. Such people regard any scientific research (or, logically, medical treatment) as unwarranted trespassing on God's prerogatives. They are of the same way of thinking as those who condemned Simpson for using chloroform during childbirth, since 'in pain (women) shall bring forth children' (Genesis 3:16). Simpson's rejoinder was to refer his critics to God's earlier use of a general anaesthetic in Genesis 2:21. However, Christian – particularly Protestant – tradition has always been on the side of enquiry as a means of understanding God's purposes better: thinking God's thoughts after him, in Kepler's phrase. Most of the founders of the Royal Society were Puritans; Isaac Newton was more interested in eschatology than physics; Rutherford caused the words 'Great are the works of the Lord, studied by all who have pleasure in them' (Psalm 111:2) to be carved over the entrance of the Cavendish Laboratory in Cambridge; the discoverer of the basic laws of genetics, Gregor Mendel, was an Augustinian abbot; and the tradition of scientific enterprise by Christians continues unabated.

Is there any particular danger in genetical experiment which may bring it under God's condemnation? Individual conscience must be the arbiter here: there are ethically sensitive areas in parts of genetical research where Christian involvement may do better by regulating than boycotting.

## Human reproduction

The techniques of artificial insemination, egg or zygote transfer, selective abortion of deformed foetuses, etc., raise several issues: a woman may bear a child carrying neither her husband's genes nor her own. This may be construed as adultery, but since her marriage was primarily designed for social and not sexual purposes (Genesis 2:18), decisions about the morality of these techniques are better based on whether or not the participants are dehumanised, *ie* reduced to the status of mere machines rather than the integrated body-mind-spirit that we are designed to be by God. A similar criterion can be applied to experiments on foetal tissue: an embryo which has no chance of developing to be a 'person' may conscientiously be used for research which may lead to the prevention of future deformity or alleviation of suffering. Notwithstanding, babies born to a couple who are not its genetical parents are technically illegitimate as the law stands at present.

Arguments are increasingly being advanced that particular couples with a high risk of producing abnormal children should not reproduce because of the burden that their offspring will place upon society. Although this is a valid factor in any decisions that are made (*eg* Amos 5:11), it is more important to consider the personal suffering of any child that might be born, and its effects on the family, including other children.

## Race

Different populations differ genetically. It has been claimed that it is degrading to study the differences because some people (or groups, or races) might be humiliated in comparison with others. This is nonsense: God has a role for each one of us, and it is better to know the innate capabilities of different people than falsely (and untheologically) assume all men are identical (Matthew 25:14–30, Mark 4:8, 1 Corinthians 12:27 *ff*, etc.).

## Microbial drug resistance

Disease-causing organisms fairly rapidly evolve resistance to drugs. Unfortunately the genes conferring resistance can sometimes be transferred to other micro-organisms, including some which are normal and usually harmless inhabitants of the gut. The mechanisms of transfer between forms, and the possibility of incorporating useful properties in strains lacking them (such as the ability to make missing enzymes in the cells of people who are inherently incapable of synthesising them) has led to much profitable research and hope for diseased people. It is possible that a virulent disease organism might be produced and propagated as a result. The chance of this happening is a subject for expert argument: many scientists think the risk is negligible if appropriate safeguards are taken, and the whole subject is now a matter for governmental control.

Ethical unease about genetical experiment probably stems from a belief that genes are sacred objects, fundamental to creation. They are not. There are a variety of problems which may arise from research in genetics, but their solution will come from the application of general principles or responsibility towards nature rather than from any special pleading or anathemata.

**R. J. Berry**

### Further reading

*Issues of Life and Death* J. N. D. Anderson (Hodder & Stoughton)
*Ethical Issues in Human Genetics* B. Hilton, D. Callaham, M. Harris, P. Condliffe & B. Berkley (eds) (Plenum)
*Our Future Inheritance: Choice or Chance?* A. Jones & W. F. Bodmer (Oxford UP)
*Science and Christian Faith Today* D. M. Mackay (Falcon)
*Fabricated Man* P. Ramsey (New Haven and London: Yale UP)

# 13
# What's the harm in sex before marriage?

Falling in love is an unforgettable experience. One day life seems to be going on in much the usual way and the next – well, the poets and the songwriters have tried to capture the champagne feeling but, honestly, can you put it in words?

Yes, but then there's the sex thing to consider as well. Marvellous when it goes right, but hell when it doesn't. Tolstoy once said that the world's greatest tragedy was the bedroom.

Put the two together – sex and falling in love – and you've got the most explosive potential known to man (feminists please add 'and woman'). The agony and the ecstasy of it, the pain and the pleasure. 'Oh, have you been in love, me boys, oh, have you felt the pain,' sang John McCormack years ago. And he went on, 'I'd sooner be in jail meself than be in love again.'

Christians, being human, are no different from anybody else when it comes to the experiences of sex and falling in love. 'If you prick us, do we not bleed?' complained Shylock on behalf of his fellow Jews. So, too, we feel our sexuality and its potency just as much as anyone else and we'd be in a much worse state if we didn't. There's nothing wrong about feeling the power of erotic love and its physical and emotional aspects.

Isn't it strange that I need to have to say that? Strange, that a Christian has to defend sexuality as a God-given thing? You open your Bible and you come to the Song of Solomon. There it is, an oriental love poem extolling the beauty of the beloved and the desirability of making love to such a wonderful person. It's there in the

Bible. Lush imagery, warm with passion, taut with unfulfilled desire.

So why is it in the Bible? Surely to show that the God who made human beings in his own image and planned that 'the two shall become one flesh' means it to be that way. How sad it is that Christians down the ages have warped it and twisted it until some of them have become ashamed even to think of their own or another's sexuality. It's high time we sang a *Te Deum* about our sexuality.

### The fool and the Fall

Right. So sex (in the sense of sexuality) is good, glorious and God-inspired. It is a part of my humanity, a great creative aspect of my being-made-in-his-image and I will not debase it into a sordid, shameful, guilt-ridden desire, to be kept under and repressed.

But the world is not short of fools. And the fools always manage to get things upside down. And the fools have really made a fine old mess of sex. On the one side are the Christian fools who come in two sizes. The first lot have ruined sex by their fear of its power. They have let fear dominate them and there have even been extremists who have castrated themselves in the hope that such a step would solve the problem.

But there's also the other kind of naïve Christian who forgets that man made in God's image is a child of what the Bible calls the 'Fall'. Christian or no, we all have the capacity to taint what we touch. We aren't perfect. We are sinners even when forgiven. 'At one and the same time,' wrote Martin Luther, 'sinners and, yet, justified.' The Christian who can't believe himself (or herself) capable of sin is in need of some hard study in John's first letter. And if sin, then sin in the field of sex is just as possible as in any other areas of life.

Of course we mustn't forget the other sorts of fools. As the Psalmist wrote, 'The fool has said to himself: "there is no God"' (Psalm 14:1). In twentieth-century Britain there are plenty of fools like that whose lives admit of no creator, no master, and so, quite logically, of no restraints upon their behaviour. For them, sex is an appetite to be satisfied as and when they wish and with whom they wish. No Christian can possibly accept their view of life or their way of living it. It is as simple as this: I am a man under authority. I am not my own master. I have been bought for an unbelievable price – the life-blood of Jesus Christ.

**Hold your horses!**

That means just this. I gladly accept that my sexuality is God-given. But I also sadly accept that my sexuality is a field ripe for self-exploitation. It's one aspect of my sinful nature. Only one. But it's still there and I dare not delude myself into forgetting it. It's not my sexuality that's shameful. It's me!

So I treat sex and all that goes with it with respect. I know it can be great as an experience. I know too that it can go wrong as an experience. But right or wrong, enjoyable or frustrating, as an experience is only one side of it. The other is the right or wrong of the actual motives and actions in moral terms. For the whole sex and falling-in-love bit needs both to be right – the experience and the morality.

Christians therefore accept what they believe to be creative restraint upon their sexuality. They don't go to bed with people at the drop of a hat (or should it be 'a skirt'?). They don't treat each other's bodies as amusement arcades – mere fun palaces. They know the way that their chemistry works and the powerful instincts which a bit of the old slap-and-tickle arouses. They are cautious about rushing into a wild embrace simply because it's enjoyable. In other words, Christians believe in marriage or, to use the language of the sociologists, in permanent pair-bonding. They see the union of two bodies sexually as the symbol of a total commitment – 'the two become one flesh' to which they add 'under one master – God.' And they keep sexual intercourse within that relationship.

**Milestones and signposts**

Get that foundation principle clear and you're on the right road to sorting out the practical questions which face every young unmarried boy or girl.

So what are the practical questions? Let's take them in the logical order:

*First question:* Are there any limitations on who I should go out with? Answer: if God is my master then I cannot contemplate a relationship with someone who refuses to accept his Lordship. That's not a petty restriction. It's an obvious part of my discipleship. And suppose I experience 'falling in love' with an unbeliever. Does that make it right? No, certainly not. After all, if I 'fall in love' with someone who's already married, it doesn't make adultery right! 'Falling in love' is not a self-validating experience. Lots of people are very prone to 'falling in love.' But my emotions alone are no sure guide to what is a right course of action. My feelings can be like a yo-yo. Only a fool lets his feelings, his moods, his emotions, become master of his actions.

*Second question:* How far can I go? As Eric Morecambe would say, 'There's no answer to that.' But there are some useful pointers. Try asking yourself whether you are doing whatever you're doing because you like *it* or because it is a genuinely appropriate action at the state which your total relationship has reached. In short, the *it* ought to be a mile-stone at the end of a part of your inter-personal journey, not the sign-post at the beginning. I've tried to spell all this out in my paperback *And so to Bed?* Why not read that?

*Last question:* Must every friendship be started with one eye on the possibility of a wedding ring? Answer: of course not. Men and women can and should learn to be good friends as Christians. But it doesn't take long to realise that once the touching starts it's better to be open with each other and sort things out or someone is sure to get hurt. Good friends don't have to be lovers (even in terms of the most minimal intimacies) but they do need to know just where each stands. That's only fair. Kisses do have a way of being misinterpreted!

Underlying it all is prayer. 'Lord, please guide me and keep me from making a fool of myself or from hurting anyone else. Please show me the way which is your way and give me courage to take it.' That kind of prayer gets answered.

When I was asked to write this I said, 'It's impossible to do justice to it in a few hundred words.' So it is. That's why I wrote *And so to Bed?* in the first place. Maybe this will give you a taste for the book. In the meantime put God first and thank him for your sexuality. Then ask him to help you to use it responsibly. That's what it's all about.

**Michael Saward**

**Further reading**
*And so to Bed?* Michael Saward (Good Reading)

# 14
# What has the Church to say about divorce and remarriage?

What indeed? Some caustic words of R. H. Tawney used in quite another connection spring to mind. 'Universities and divines,' he remarked, 'gave, as is their wont, a loud, but confused, response' (*Religion and the Rise of Capitalism* (Pelican)). So our main concern must be to find what Scripture says.

## The Creator's answer
God has expressed himself very bluntly on both divorce and remarriage. On the first of these he puts it in three words, 'I hate divorce.' On the second he says that whoever divorces husband or wife and remarries 'commits adultery.' See Malachi 2:16, Mark 10:11, 12.

If this sounds sweeping, remember that the way we are made is already pointing in this direction, since we hardly need the Bible to tell us that men and women are not *things* to be scrapped as soon as they cease to please ('Trade in your husband/wife for this year's model'); and the fact that the sexes are – in more ways than one – a match for each other suggests that a married couple will need time and patience to achieve anything like a mature relationship. It is also well known that the children of a marriage depend on their parents too long and too deeply to come out unhurt from a domestic break-up – particularly as their very dependence tends to make them a centre of dispute, the rope in the parental tug-of-war.

But the Bible takes all this much further by showing that we exist for God, stamped with his likeness. It follows that much more is at stake than one's private or even shared convenience and happiness: what *God* wishes becomes the first and last question on the subject.

## The Old Testament

God's design for marriage is laid down at the outset of the Bible (Genesis 2:18–25). Moreover, Jesus appealed to this pattern as basic for all time. It shows the first man and woman as divinely-planned companions, each the complement of the other (for the famous expression 'a help meet' means just this). The whole interest of the story of Eve's creation is in this personal partnership; and in case we should miss the point, a line is drawn straight from Eden to every marriage, in the words 'Therefore shall a man . . . cleave unto his wife and they shall be one flesh.' These are the words Jesus quoted.

So the first and final sayings of the Old Testament on the marriage-bond reinforce one another, and both are based on the concept of partnership. '. . . she is your companion,' says God through Malachi, 'and your wife by covenant.' Yet the middle pages have a different look, for divorce was taken for granted in the law of Moses; and at one time of crisis it was even commanded, in order to undo a tangle of foreign marriages which was choking the Jewish community of Ezra's day. So it is hardly surprising that the legal experts whom we meet in the Gospels were debating not *whether* divorce was allowable, but only what made it so.

## The New Testament

Jesus, as ever, pierced straight to the essentials. To him the Law was not a set of regulations to be studied for loopholes, but the voice of God about practical truth and love. In the Sermon on the Mount (see Matthew 5:27–32) before he mentioned divorce he spoke of adultery, and in both cases he made us look at the realities of our behaviour, not the legal niceties – for we may be comfortably within the law in our acts and right outside it in our thoughts; or unassailable on our rights and damnable in our relationships.

But in Matthew 19 he went further still. He pointed out that marriage involves you with your Creator. It is his work you pull apart when you get a divorce. Jesus put it unforgettably, in a phrase the Marriage Service has borrowed for its moment of climax: 'What . . . God has joined together, let no man put asunder' (Matthew 19:6). So the whole thrust of his teaching is towards the level at which you are shamed out of tampering with so high a matter, and divorce appears as an outrage against man and God.

## One exception

Yet the Old Testament had provided for divorce and remarriage, even while it spoke against it; and Jesus defended this on the simple ground that men must be governed and laws must be workable. In fact he went further, for he made one exception himself to his absolute prohibition, puncturing it by the clause 'except for unchastity,' reported twice by Matthew (5:32, 19:9). So the New Testament like the Old seems to speak with two voices. What are we to make of it?

Certainly we must make no more of it than the New Testament does. The exception is almost invisible: Mark and Luke give no hint of it, and Matthew in reporting it makes it clear that it did nothing to lessen the disciples' shock at the high standard Jesus was setting. 'If that is the position,' they exclaimed, 'it is better to refrain from marriage.' It was the *principle* that had registered with them, not the exception.

Second, Jesus confined this exception to the one sin, unchastity, which touches the unique relation of husband and wife. Other sins can destroy companionship and make separation advisable – always in hope of reconciliation (Paul provides for exactly this in 1 Corinthians 7:10–11), but only unchastity can strike at the married state itself. So the unique exception highlights the unique relation: it says, as strongly as the rest of the teaching, that one's partner is not for sharing.

Third, Jesus saw in the Old Testament divorce law the truth about man, not about marriage. The creation story shows what marriage is; the divorce law only what mankind has become. The same can be said of Jesus's own teaching: the very fact that unchastity has to be mentioned in the same breath as marriage proves that 'the hardness of your hearts' is nothing obsolete. If it must be provided for, that is our shame, not our right.

Finally, the whole force of God's example, as well as his words, is towards an unswerving fidelity. God's people, his bride, may have deserved divorce a thousand times; they have had his reclaiming love instead. This is why, exception or no exception, the Christian Church sees divorce and remarriage as virtually unthinkable, a contradiction (in all but a tiny minority of cases) of the love which 'bears all things, believes all things, hopes all things, endures all things.' This is the love we have received; this is what, on our infinitely smaller scale, we must give.

**Derek Kidner**

**Further reading**
*Divorce* John Stott (Falcon)

# 15
# Do Christians frustrate God's will by practising contraception?

We can conveniently consider this by asking five further questions on specific points.

## In the beginning

*Were not Adam (Genesis 1:28) and Noah (Genesis 9:1) instructed to be fruitful and multiply and replenish the earth?*
Yes, but they were on an empty planet. Since then the earth has been plenished to such an irresponsible degree that the most frightening problem facing it is not atomic weaponry but the population explosion.

The divine command then continued 'and subdue it.' Nature is to be subdued. God said to Eve, 'I will greatly multiply ... thy conception' (Genesis 3:16). The Hebrew allows us to take this at its face value. Hyperfertility may indeed be one of the curses of the fall which we can legitimately tackle as we have tackled the companion curse of weeds by our agricultural methods, and of painful labour with our analgesic techniques.

Today when tens of millions of children in the third world are starving it is increasingly obvious that to be pro-life may demand being anti-birth. In these underdeveloped lands today it is often true that to permit an addition to the family is to pronounce a death-sentence on the present youngest child.

## The chief end of marriage

*Solomon tells us that 'Sons are a heritage from the Lord, and children are a reward from him. . . . Happy is the man who has his quiver full of them' (Psalm 127:3, 5). Should we not accept as many children as God sends?*

Marriage was ordained by God for the mutual companionship of man and woman. We are told three times, 'Therefore shall a man leave his father and his mother and shall cleave unto his wife and they shall be one flesh.' Walter Trobisch comments that on each occasion the text ends with a full stop: there is no mention of children (*I Married You*). While the blessing of children is stressed repeatedly in Scripture, their production is not the chief end of marriage. That primary purpose is impossible, in the view of many people, if children arrive in annual succession.

Rosemary Ruether, a Roman Catholic, has written: 'We come to the ironic fact that in our present situation man is only able fully to say "yes" to procreation if he is also able to say "no"' (*Contraception and Holiness: the Catholic Predicament*). For in almost every marriage however much the parents love children, there comes a time when the wife knows that her resources of time, of strength, of emotional response, of money, will not stretch to provide adequately for another child. No doubt if one arrived they would get by, but she is aware that at best this could be achieved only by some deprivation in affection and care. Knowing this she can act responsibly only by avoiding conception. In the past this could be achieved only by encasing herself in an armour of emotional unresponsiveness. In other words she was in a dilemma: she either had to deny her union with her husband in one flesh, or her role as mother. Today however she has the option of continuing her close relationship with her husband, and at the same time of fulfilling her call to be homemaker, by employing contraception.

## Frustrating God's plans?

*As some of God's messengers have been aware that he chose them before birth (Isaiah 49:1, Jeremiah 1:5, Galatians 1:15), may we not unwittingly frustrate God's plans by preventing conception?*

First we have to realise that God *must* overrule even when conception is planned. It is not widely known that the production of the male sperm is so vast that at any one normal act of intercourse there are about two hundred million different possibilities as to the genetic character of the baby to be initiated. Sperm competition is such that the child conceived at 11 o'clock is different from that which would have been conceived twenty minutes earlier. Once conceived there is a great, perhaps even 50% chance that the pregnancy will not proceed successfully, most of these losses occurring so early that the woman never realises that the egg had been fertilized. If despite all this, God is able, as we believe, to achieve his purposes we do not need to fear that our decisions will upset his plans. By the same token, abstinence from intercourse, whether in marriage or by celibacy, powerfully limits God's freedom of action.

### Leaving results to the Lord?

*Is it right to use artificial means? Why not practise normal intercourse and leave the results to the Lord?*
This sounds very spiritual. There are few however who advocate such reliance when it comes to other spheres of life. We wear safety belts, we take out insurance policies. Those of us who are parents ensure that our child's milk supply is bacteria free, that the family have an artificially purified water supply, that if they are liable to infection they are artificially supplied with artificial protection in the form of inoculation or vaccination or prophylaxis. If we are ill, we take the appropriate drug. The population problem arises today because we have practised death-control. Were we wrong? Should we allow four out of five of our children to succumb to disease in their first months, or should we protect them by every artificial means at our disposal – and thank God who has made these means available?

It should be noted that God withdrew his miraculous supply of manna as soon as the Israelites were in a position to look to their own food supplies.

### Sterilisation

*Is it right to be sterilised?*
Sterilisation is surgically produced contraception which should be considered as virtually irreversible. Where there is a medical reason why the married woman should not have any more children it would appear to be a wise step. Also if there is a strong possibility of an

abnormal child resulting from a genetic anomaly in either parent, that parent may consider sterilisation.

Problems arise in people's minds as to whether they should be sterilised when they feel they have completed their family. In a situation where all other methods of contraception have been tried and have failed, there is a clear case for sterilisation. However, many Christians have opted for sterilisation even where other methods were available to them. In our judgement each couple must decide together what is right for them, but we would strongly advise against the operation if either partner has any reservations.

Perhaps the most powerful argument in favour of the use of a trusted contraceptive technique is that in our clinical experience we have found that any other course leads to tensions and frustrations in the marriage, tensions which spill over adversely to affect the children. It is irrelevant to consider what might have been the course to which God called his servants in a different age. He has placed us in an age where contraceptives are available, where child survival has been artificially and beneficially manipulated by science. It is in such an age that we have been called to manifest his life, and to accept his provision with thankfulness.

**R. F. R. Gardner**
**Elizabeth S. Gardner**

# 16

# Should a Christian ever consider an abortion?—I
## *A GP's view*

Let us first be clear what is meant by abortion and what it involves. Abortion is the ending of a pregnancy before its 28th week; it is only beyond this stage of development that a child born alive is considered capable of a separate successful existence. Modern medicine however has enabled babies born even four weeks earlier to survive. In future years further advances might be made and the child of such an early birth may well be able to continue to adult life. So there is no fixed stage of development beyond which a child born alive will be able to survive, and inevitably fail to do so if born earlier.

### The unborn child
'Legal' abortion is usually done in the 13th to 18th week of pregnancy, or even a little later. The legally aborted child, had it been born alive spontaneously instead of being deliberately destroyed, could under appropriate conditions have survived for a little time. With improved paediatric techniques the child at this stage of development may, in years to come, also be able to survive even to manhood.

At the time when most legal abortions are carried out the child in the womb has all obvious essentials for continuing existence. It moves, reacts to painful stimuli, its heart beats, it urinates, and in appearance is a complete miniature human child. Though lying in the womb, it is no part of the mother, and has its own independent blood system. Since conception it has been a separate individual, genetically different from either parent, and in fact is entirely parasitic on its mother, absorbing its requirements from her blood supply through its placenta.

Thus abortion, the killing of a small live separate individual human being, whether done within the law or not, is murder before birth, just as much as it would be murder if the child were destroyed after birth.

## The Christian view

Human life for Christians is the on-going process of our creation by God. It is sinful to take human life; so for a Christian human abortion is also as sinful. The respect for human life shown by a Christian should include removal of anything endangering life; it is as culpable passively to let human life be destroyed, as it is actively to destroy it.

When a pregnancy imperils the mother's life, there is the dilemma of balancing the life of the mother against that of her unborn child. To remove the child at a stage when it could not survive – that is by abortion – inevitably means killing the child. Some Christians would leave the solution to God; but many other Christians would consider that, being endowed with intelligence and free will, it would be reasonable for them to protect the mother's life, if she wishes, by aborting the pregnancy.

Another problem arises when it is known that the child will be born abnormal. Some Christians would consider this justification for abortion, thereby compassionately sparing the mother the burden of bearing and bringing up such a child. But an abnormal child in a family need not be a tragedy; there are many examples of such children uniting members of their family in Christian compassion, to give them happy lives. The social services can also give great support. It should also be remembered that serious, permanent, handicapping abnormality can strike any member of a family, child or otherwise, as the result of illness or accident, and there can be no question of murder then. Many Christians would not consider abnormality of the unborn child as justification for abortion. But there can be gross abnormality in an unborn child that would rob it of individual existence, for example the anencephalic without brain. Most Christians would accept abortion in such a case.

Thus many Christians would justify abortion in those instances where the mother's life seems to be imperilled by the pregnancy, or her health, physical and mental, appears in danger of serious permanent damage, or the unborn child is likely to be born very seriously abnormal. But such abortion is nevertheless sinful. To some Christians it seems justifiable; but not so to others.

## Social cases

The 1967 Abortion Act permits abortion in the categories already mentioned, but in addition sanctions it where the lives of the existing children of the family would seem endangered by the advent of another child, in their existing or reasonably foreseeable environment. This is a social matter; it is for society to ensure that one more child does not imperil the lives of a family. Murder of a normal unborn child is no more solution than it would be after birth.

## Other considerations

Arguments have been advanced for abortion in a variety of other circumstances which aggregate to a plea for abortion on demand. First, the *unwanted*. It can happen that the unwanted pregnancy does not lead to an unwanted child, when it arrives. On the contrary, such a baby is often well loved. But this is not always so and we must be aware of the hardships which sometimes face such a child.

In the case of the lone mother certain social and economic considerations arise. Illegitimacy is no longer a social stigma. Many women whether married or not bring up their children alone, but not nearly enough is done to help these women with their practical difficulties. Society has a duty to help solve their problems, but not to liquidate them. Single women with children can and do marry happily, as do widows and the divorced.

Whether a *child* is made to feel unwanted depends on the personality of the mother, married or single. It is her responsibility. Unwanted pregnancy in itself is no justification for abortion.

## Women's rights

Next are the abortions labelled as women's rights. It is claimed sensibly that every woman has the right to control her fertility; but such a failure is one of the risks which has to be accepted in sexual relations, and leads on to the unwanted pregnancy – a social matter, not a case for abortion. It is also said that every woman has the right to decide what she will do with her body. If this is true for any person, it still does not give a woman the right to destroy the living body of another individual, the child she helped to put into her womb. Another version is that if it is permissible to remove an offending part of the body, such as a troublesome appendix, tooth or tonsil, the same should apply to a pregnancy. But this is not a valid comparison, as the unborn child is no *part* of the mother's body, but is a *separate body*. One strange theory is that a doctor who does not agree to abort a pregnancy is forcing the mother to carry the child to full term against her will! Every doctor must be free to act according to his conscience. It is the patient who has put herself in the position of *having* to carry the pregnancy.

**Conclusion**

When abortion is considered, there is often reference to the rights of the individual and to Christian compassion. The unborn child has the right to go on living, and is worthy of Christian compassion.

One should not try to judge people. Those directly concerned in an abortion, if they are Christians, are making their decision before God; he is the only judge. Those who have no faith cannot be measured by Christian standards. Likewise those who are not directly concerned in an abortion decision should not judge those who are. They cannot know the full and real circumstances. Should they be directly involved one day, they may find that their preconceived ideals slip under stress.

It is said by some that it is unfair that it is the woman who is left holding the baby. Motherhood is to the vast majority of women a privilege they would not give up, even if they did not come to it readily in the first place.

**Walter Hedgcock**

# 17
# Should a Christian ever consider an abortion?—II
*A gynaecologist's view*

In modern life, circumstances and problems arise about which the Bible does not seem to give specific guidance: but general principles are given, which can be applied prayerfully to every situation. Abortion is one such problem, involving theological, moral, legal and physical issues, and causing much distress to individuals and families. Whenever emotive factors influence decisions, the Christian can only hope to make right decisions by adhering to biblical principles.

## The value of human life
What value does God place on human life? – High enough to create a world of beauty for man to live in, and to give his Son, Jesus Christ, to save him! Psalm 139 shows that God is concerned about the development of the foetus (verses 13–16 – 'Thou didst knit me together in my mother's womb ... my frame was not hidden from thee when I was being made in secret.... Thy eyes beheld my unformed substance ...') and the sixth Commandment states 'Thou shalt not kill' (Exodus 20:13). Therefore, should deliberate termination of foetal life ever be performed? The Roman Catholic Church says 'no,' not even in the rare circumstances when the mother's life is endangered.

## The historical background
Historically, the aim of Medicine has always been to preserve life,

and we know that in Greco-Roman times, *ie*, pre-Christian, abortion was sometimes practised, but the physician taking the Hippocratic Oath (*c*.400 BC) swore not to do so. In England this standard applied throughout the Middle Ages, and in 1861, the *Offence against the Person Act* stated that it was a felony to procure, or attempt to procure, an *unlawful abortion*, and a convicted person was liable to be sentenced to penal servitude for life, with or without hard labour. In 1929, the *Infant Life Preservation Act* stated that 'child destruction' of a foetus after 28 weeks was a felony equivalent to murder or manslaughter, unless done in good faith for the purpose only of preserving the life of the mother.

In the *Rex* v. *Bourne Case of 1938*, the gynaecologist was acquitted after aborting a fourteen-year-old girl, pregnant following rape, on the grounds that this was a *lawful* abortion in the terms of the 1861 Act: in the following years, 'case precedent' was the basis for abortions performed when the mother's life or health was thought to be greatly at risk.

The Abortion Law Reform Society and similar organisations fought to 'liberalise' the Abortion Laws, on the grounds of presumed large numbers of backstreet abortions, and the medical profession agreed that clarification of the law would be advantageous but did not want to see the introduction of abortion on demand, for medical as well as ethical reasons.

## 1967 Abortion Act

Now the situation in England, since the *1967 Abortion Act*, is that abortion is permissible under four circumstances only, *viz*, if:

1  the continuance of the pregnancy would involve risk to the life of the pregnant woman greater than if the pregnancy were terminated;
2  the continuance of the pregnancy would involve risk of injury to the physical or mental health of the pregnant woman greater than if the pregnancy were terminated;
3  the continuance of the pregnancy would involve risk of injury to the physical or mental health of the existing child(ren) of the family of the pregnant woman greater than if the pregnancy were terminated;
4  there is substantial risk that if the child were born it would suffer from such physical or mental abnormalities as to be seriously handicapped.

Clause 1 is rarely applicable now, except in suicidal patients, as pregnancy in most medical conditions does not endanger the *life* of the mother. Most patients fall into the group covered by Clause 2, and it is the responsibility of two doctors to decide how much the mother's *health*, physical or mental, will be adversely affected by the pregnancy, and whether this constitutes grounds for terminating the pregnancy or not. Obviously there will be individual variation of opinion on this, to some extent coloured (perhaps unconsciously) by a doctor's own moral views on abortion, and there can be no hard and fast rules when making a *clinical* judgement.

Clause 3 is often termed a *social* clause, and many gynaecologists feel that abortion is not the answer to poor social conditions, although the unplanned pregnancy may well make them almost intolerable – but better housing, etc. should be available through the welfare services and the patient given advice about family planning, or offered sterilisation, to prevent a repetition of the problem.

Clause 4 is employed more frequently now as methods of diagnosing foetal abnormality early in the pregnancy become available, and amniocentesis (examination of the water surrounding the foetus) is employed routinely if the mother is aged over forty years because of the increasing risk of Down's syndrome (mongolism) or if there is a family history of brain or spinal cord abnormalities, such as anencephaly or spina bifida. Termination of pregnancy is often performed if the mother contracts rubella (German measles) very early in the pregnancy, as the development of the heart, eyes or inner ears of the foetus may be impaired. Certain of these malformations are not incompatible with some degree of normal life, but often one cannot foretell this, and how does one convert a statistical risk in a familial, but nondiagnosable, disease to an individual patient seeking advice on whether her pregnancy should be terminated or not?

Thus the Christian faces a conflict, whether as the mother of an unplanned pregnancy or as a gynaecologist whose advice is asked, and who also has a responsibility to the country's National Health Service which employs him. At present a *conscience clause* allows a gynaecologist to opt out of doing abortions, but this throws a heavier work load on his colleagues and presents variations in the availability of abortion under the NHS in different parts of the country. Selection Committees appointing consultants have already had directives from the Department of Health and Social Security suggesting that the candidates' willingness to do abortions should be a factor to be considered when they are applying for posts in a conservative area.

Does the timing of when the foetus receives its *soul* (or rather, *spirit*) help one to decide whether abortion in the very early stages can be acceptable or not? The Bible is silent on this point, but I have found it helpful in my own consultant practice to think of the value of the individual to God – and likewise of the *potential* individual, whether he receives his *soul* at conception or later. If one says *at conception*, there is the problem of the many thousands of spontaneous, extremely early abortions when the foetus is still incompletely formed, but if one says *later* there is difficulty in fixing the exact time: is it the moment of *viability* (which varies with advances of medical science and their availability) or not until *birth*, when the foetus becomes an independent individual? I feel that this dilemma does not detract from the main principle of respect for *life* and *potential life*, and abortion is rarely justified except in the presence of grave maternal illness, either physical or mental, and should not be done for trivial reasons or used as a form of contraception.

There are good medical justifications for this view too. The *British Medical Journal* of 10th July 1976, quoting the Report on Confidential Enquiries into Maternal Deaths, 1970–72, points out that abortion remains the most common cause of death associated with pregnancy. Previously, this was mainly following illegal abortion, but now equally following illegal and legal abortions, *viz*, in 1952–4, total deaths were 153 (108 after illegal, 43 after spontaneous and 2 after legal abortions) and in 1970–72, total deaths were 81 (38 after illegal, 6 after spontaneous and 37 after legal abortions). The number of legal abortions in 1975 in England and Wales was more than 140,000, 106,000 of which were on residents. The Lane Committee, appointed to investigate the working of the 1967 Abortion Act, reported in 1974, and a Select Committee is now sitting, following the Private Member's Abortion Amendment Bill, which was before the House of Commons in 1975; so further legislation is possible.

Abortion is but one aspect of life in a permissive society, and the Christian should make every effort to be an influence for good in society. With regard to the individual needing help, Christ's principle of compassion should be paramount, but tempered with his command 'Go and do not sin again' (John 8:11) where applicable.

**Eunice R. Burton**

**Further reading**

*What about Abortion?* Rex Gardner (Paternoster Press)
*Abortion: the Personal Dilemma* Rex Gardner (Paternoster Press)
*Biblical Allusions to Life before Birth* Harley Smyth (Christian Medical Fellowship)
*The Christian and the Unborn Child* Oliver O'Donovan (Grove Booklets on Ethics, includes Text of Abortion Act, 1967)
*What's Wrong with Abortion* J. J. Scarisbrick (Life)

# 18

# Can we accept a homosexual as a Christian?

There are few subjects that arouse such violent and emotional reactions as homosexuality. And as with most discussions of this kind, the homosexuality debate tends to generate more heat than light. Those on both sides of the argument are sometimes guilty of misunderstanding the facts, and the confusion that results is to nobody's advantage. It will be helpful, then, to begin with one or two important distinctions.

## Some distinctions

*Perverts and inverts*
The pervert is a man or woman who is basically heterosexual in orientation, but dabbles in homosexual behaviour for variety, curiosity or kicks. Inverts, by contrast, are people who have never known what it is to be attracted to members of the opposite sex. For them, homosexual attraction seems perfectly natural. Many observers bracket all homosexuality with perversion. That is unfair and confusing. The vast majority of all homosexuals are inverts, and their numbers are significant – possibly as high as one in twenty-five of the total population.

*Sex and gender*
Sex is something determined at birth; it is anatomically obvious to

midwife and mother whether a new-born baby is a boy or a girl. Gender, on the other hand, is a far more complex matter. It has to do with feelings, attitudes, tastes and character.

Encouraged by the media, and especially by the advertisers, we tend to distinguish sharply between an approach to life which is essentially masculine and a list of character-traits and attitudes which are labelled feminine. Unfortunately, not all those who have the genital apparatus of one sex fall into the 'right' side of the gender divide. Some 'men' find themselves trapped in female bodies, and vice versa. It could well be that many people *feel* themselves to be invert homosexuals when what they really mean is that they fail to share the feelings and characteristics of their sex, as set out in the glossy periodicals.

*Feelings and conduct*
By no means all inverts practise as homosexuals. Many try to suppress their feelings. Some get married and have children in a desperate attempt to appear 'normal' in a world that is still hostile to homosexuality. When we talk about accepting homosexuals, we have to distinguish between those who feel that way, and those who act on their feelings.

*Sex and friendship*
This is a vital distinction which is difficult to draw. A kiss, an embrace, or even a handshake may be the prelude to a sex-union or a mark of friendship, depending on the circumstances and the attitudes of those who give and receive the gesture. It is important to distinguish homosexual behaviour from physical expressions of friendship which are wholesome and right.

At this point social pressures may influence our attitudes more strongly than we think. Englishmen are not surprised when they see two girl friends exchange a kiss in the street, but they are horrified if they notice two boys doing the same. On the other side of the English Channel, men embrace warmly and nobody minds. Our differences of social outlook must be taken into account if our moral judgements are not to be clouded.

*Immorality and disgust*
This point follows closely on the last. It is all too easy for us to label things we find distasteful as immoral. But not everything that

nauseates us is morally wrong. The sight of a man eating raw eggs may make me sick, but he has not acted immorally just because I do not like what he does.

This is a distinction we must be particularly careful to draw when we judge behaviour between two people of the same sex. Most heterosexuals find the very thought of homosexual conduct disturbing if not disgusting – but that *alone* does not make it immoral.

*One-night stands and a lasting union*
It is always a mistake to dismiss other people's opinions by caricaturing them. Homosexual behaviour is often bracketed with promiscuity and condemned for much the same reasons. The charge sometimes sticks, because lasting homosexual unions seem particularly difficult to achieve. But it would be quite wrong to assume that all homosexuals only seek partners for occasional physical gratification. Many sincerely desire a lasting bond in which sex plays a minor role. We may still believe that such a life-style is wrong, but we must be careful not to condemn it in the same breath as we decry a one-night stand with a prostitute.

## So is it wrong?
Distinctions of this kind underlie the insistent appeals we hear today for a more liberal approach to homosexuality. If some people are so made that they can only form an intimate relationship with a member of their own sex, why should they be denied something the heterosexual majority freely enjoy? Modern scientific knowledge has helped us to understand the invert homosexual. Now is the time, we are told, to convert understanding into acceptance by revising our civil and moral law-codes, to allow homosexuals to fulfil themselves in the only way they know how.

On both sides of the Atlantic prominent churchmen echo these sentiments. Jesus, they remind us, summed up all moral values under the heading of love. How, then, can it be wrong for two people who care for one another genuinely, and who intend to stand by one another for life, to express their affection through the physical channels God has given them?

## The Bible's view
Jesus used his Bible to unpack the true meaning of love, and we must do the same. At no time did he hint that a loving motive could make a

wrong thing right. It is important therefore to sift out the Bible's teaching on homosexuality in order to find out whether a 'gay' relationship can ever be acceptable in God's sight.

Whenever the Bible mentions homosexuality, it bans it. What is not always so clear, however, is whether *all* homosexual relationships come under the biblical veto.

The Sodom incident, for example (described in Genesis 19; *cf* Judges 19:14–28), demonstrates the extremely serious view God takes of all homosexual assault – but it says nothing about the rightness or wrongness of a tender homosexual relationship where there is full consent on both sides. The law of Moses goes further by condemning homosexual behaviour alongside adultery and incest (either of which may involve a love-bond), but it uses a word (*abomination*) which is normally reserved for idolatry (Leviticus 18:22, 20:13). In other words, God's judgement on assault and idolatry is clear. But does he also condemn a homosexual relationship where there is no attempt by one partner to force his (or her) favours on the other, and no desire to worship false gods?

Some find these doubts reflected in the New Testament's teaching. Paul is very blunt in outlawing homosexuality in his letters to the church at Corinth (1 Corinthians 6:9) and to young Timothy in Ephesus (1 Timothy 1:10). He also condemns, in the strongest language, those who have 'exchanged natural relations for unnatural' (Romans 1:26). But do his stern words apply to the invert as well as the pervert? The invert homosexual may well feel he has no such 'natural' relations to exchange.

The doctrinal foundations on which Paul builds his teaching sweep all such doubts and hesitations aside. In Romans, his verdict on homosexuality is based on *God's creation plan* for man and woman. By 'natural relations' he means 'natural to man and woman as God created them' – and homosexuality played no part in the Creator's scheme. In 1 Timothy, the condemnation of practising homosexuals is built into Paul's own updated version of the *Ten Commandments*; and those commandments, as we know, reflect the main principles of creation as they are outlined for us in Genesis. It comes as no surprise to find that in 1 Corinthians the veto on homosexual conduct occurs in a list of behaviour-patterns which find no place in *God's kingdom* – where the Creator's will is perfectly done.

The conclusion is unmistakable. Deeper foundations could hardly be laid for biblical teaching on any subject. Modern distinctions, important though they are, are undercut. The New Testament puts an emphatic ban on all homosexual behaviour.

## A final distinction

There seems no reasonable doubt that homosexual conduct must be clearly labelled as sin. But the Bible distinguishes sharply between sin and the sinner. Everyone has weaknesses of some sort, and homosexual tendencies are not to be put in some special class of their own. As sinners, we all need the support of other Christians, and homosexuals need this supportive fellowship more than most because loneliness is their worst enemy. Some fear that the danger of ostracism, if they own up to their feelings in a Christian fellowship, is too great a risk to run. Where this is true, the church bears a large measure of blame.

God accepts us as we are, and his church can hardly do less. But God also seeks to change us, and again the homosexual is no exception to the rule. Some Christian homosexuals find that their whole sexual orientation undergoes a radical change when they open their lives to God's power. Others have to fight the same old temptations, in God's strength, all their lives. But, as many heterosexual men and women have found, the single life is not a second-best if it is part of God's will. Jesus himself lived a perfectly fulfilled human life, even though he never married.

**David Field**

**Further reading**
*Homosexuality* D. J. West (Pelican)
*The Homosexual Way – A Christian Option?* David Field (Grove Books)

# 19
# Is euthanasia necessarily wrong in all circumstances?

The word 'euthanasia' means, literally, 'dying well' and, so far as derivation is concerned, it could have been used for a policy of helping people to die in dignity and peace. But it has come to have the narrower meaning of the deliberate ending of life by a doctor. There is, nevertheless, a connection between the two, for those who favour euthanasia in the narrower sense do so because they believe that the only way to ensure a peaceful and dignified death in a significant number of cases is for the doctor to take steps to end the patient's life *with his consent*. No responsible body of opinion advocates involuntary euthanasia. Since such deliberate killing would, as the law now stands, constitute murder, discussion has centred on proposals to legalise voluntary euthanasia.

## The use of drugs
Very often the demand that people 'should be allowed to die in peace' is not a demand that their lives should be deliberately ended, but rather that doctors should not persist in troublesome treatments when they can no longer do any good, but instead should concentrate upon making their patients as comfortable as possible as they prepare for death. This may mean using pain-killing drugs even at some risk of accelerating death (although it often happens that the relief of pain itself prolongs life). As such, it is a normal part of good medical practice, and much of the concern which at present expresses itself in

the demand for voluntary euthanasia would be met if people felt sure that they would not be kept alive unnecessarily and would be allowed to die in quiet and human dignity.

The ethical problem concerns not this but the deliberate taking of the patient's life. The two main arguments advanced in favour of voluntary euthanasia are:

● that compassion requires it as, in some instances, the only way of relieving severe pain;

● that the individual has a right to decide for himself whether he shall live or die, and to be medically assisted, if he chooses to die.

## The right to die

Of the two arguments the latter is the more difficult for a Christian to accept. It ascribes to the individual a degree of sovereignty over his life which it is not easy to reconcile with his duty to God and his neighbour. If a man receives his life as a gift from God, can he regard himself as free to dispose of it as he wills, even if he has satisfied himself that others will not suffer? And *can* he be sure of that?

People are not isolated individuals; they exist in a whole network of personal relationships – with family, friends and acquaintances of all kinds, including doctors and nurses; and these relationships are often subtler and stronger than the individual realises. Recognition of a right to die would, moreover, imply a duty on the part of others (including, of course, doctors and nurses and members of all the caring professions) to refrain from giving the succour which all their instincts and training prompt them to supply.

The claims of compassion cannot be gainsaid by the Christian and it is, indeed, possible to conceive of extreme cases in which to take life might be the only way of showing compassion. For example, it may be right in conditions of war to shoot severely wounded soldiers rather than allow them to die alone and untended, if there is no other way of helping them. Such tragic decisions may on occasion be inescapable, but what makes them tragic is that those who take them are compelled to violate deep convictions which they know to be an essential part of their humanity.

These extreme cases cannot provide a justification for our abandoning those convictions in the ordinary conduct of life. Compassion for the dying and incurably sick is normally and naturally shown by constant and careful attention to their needs and by staying with them in their dying. This means, in practice, an acceptance of death by all who attend the dying, as well as by the dying themselves, and a readiness to take practical means to help them make their peace with men and with God.

## The sanctity of life

In order for this to be possible there must exist an underlying confidence in society as a whole that its resources will be used for the healing of the sick and, where that is no longer possible, for the comfort of the dying, and that no one will be allowed to fall outside this care or be regarded as no longer of any worth.

This is what the principle of the 'Sanctity of Life' means in effect; and although at first sight it might appear that an accepted practice of voluntary euthanasia in a minority of cases would leave this principle unaffected, it is hard to believe that it would not in the end profoundly modify attitudes, both public and private. It would sow doubt in place of confidence and uncertainty in place of trust, and those most affected would be those who were least able to cope with these conditions. Even the independent and 'autonomous' intellectual, sure of his ground and able to think the matter through, might well become hesitant and confused as the time approached for his previous decision in favour of euthanasia to be given effect. Many, who had taken no such decision, might retain merely an obscure recollection of its possibility and become in consequence troubled and insecure.

So the Christian cannot be satisfied with simple opposition to proposals for voluntary euthanasia. He must recognise the fears and respect the concern for people which often lie behind them, and seek to relieve the fears and develop the concern by a positive policy of medical and spiritual care of the dying.

**Basil Mitchell**

**Further reading**
*On Dying Well* An Anglican contribution to the debate on euthanasia (Church Information Office)
*The Patient as Person* Paul Ramsey, ch 3 (Yale University Press)
*Dying* John Hinton (Pelican)

## 20

# Is capital punishment defensible?

This question should really start further back. Is *any* punishment defensible? – for punishment, properly speaking, is an act of retribution, and this word has few supporters now. We may feel that it should be replaced by the concept of reform, or at most, the protection of society and the deterring of other wrongdoers.

### Retribution
But retribution deserves a closer look. For a start, God's own judgement is retributive. In a famous sentence, 'he will render to every man according to his works' (Romans 2:6); and this is a doctrine which Jesus repeatedly endorsed (*eg* Matthew 25:31–46; Luke 12:41–48; John 5:25–29).

Then again, retribution is our only link with justice in this area, for it is asking what you have *done* and what you *deserve*, in deciding what is to be done about you. The other approaches can skip these questions and go straight to your thought-reform or to the good of the cause ('that the whole nation perish not', as Caiaphas remarked in deciding against Jesus).

But a frequent objection to retribution by human agents is that we are all guilty. True, we say, society must protect itself, but if it starts paying back offenders in their own coin ('a tooth for a tooth') it has the wrong attitude altogether. Didn't Jesus say as much?

He did, but not to those who administer the law. He condemned the attitude of tit-for-tat, but he had no quarrel with a ruler's right to punish. The disciple, as Paul insists in Romans 12:19, must not pay back an injury, for retribution is God's affair. But it is also, he goes on, a ruler's affair, indeed his duty, for God has delegated it to him. Romans 13:4, which makes this point, uses the same set of terms to speak up for public retribution (literally 'a retributor for wrath') as the earlier verses used against our private resort to it. (The NEB brings this out better than RSV.)

The next thing to ask is what penalty the Bible fixed for murder, and what force this may have now. The first part is soon answered. For mankind in general, from the days of Noah, God's rule was, 'Whoever sheds the blood of man, by man shall his blood be shed' (Genesis 9:6). The law of Moses reaffirmed it for Israel (*eg*, Numbers 35:29–34), and the New Testament upheld the right of a state to enact it (*eg*, Acts 25:11; Romans 13:4).

But in answer to the second question, the civil laws of the Old Testament are not carried straight over into the New. They reveal unchangeable truths – in this case, the sanctity of life, the deserts of a murderer, and society's duty to punish him – but they embody them in local regulations which are no longer binding on us just as they stand. So it is up to each state to create its own laws, but their values must stand the test of scripture.

With that in mind, we can – at last! – look at some pros and cons of capital punishment.

**Pros and cons**
Firstly let us take some points in its favour:
● It is at least legitimate, perhaps even mandatory, being prescribed in the Old Testament and unquestioned in the New
● It is based on retribution, which is a biblical principle
● It puts a high value on the victim's life (Genesis 9:6b)
● It is the strongest of deterrents (*cf* Deuteronomy 19:20)
   Against these we must place other considerations:
● Many laws, appropriate once, are now outgrown and unthinkable. Slavery, though permitted rather than commanded, is one such: death for adultery or for defiance of one's parents (Deuteronomy 21:18 *ff*) is another. Should we not add to these, death for a murderer?
● Even as retribution, this penalty is inexact; it is also irrevocable. Other sentences can match the degrees of guilt, and be revoked if necessary. So justice itself, to say nothing of mercy, seems better served by other means than death.

● The state's refusal to kill even the guilty declares the value it sets on *all* human life.

● A deterrent effect is hard to prove or to isolate from other factors. And the drama of a death sentence can even attract some whom it should repel.

## A personal summing up

Both positions have their strengths and weaknesses. Both are defensible, and the changing state of society may make one or the other the right choice for different times and places. To me, the balance falls in favour of including capital punishment in the range of sentences for the following reasons, corresponding to the pros and cons above.

Firstly, it is granted that many laws and customs are rightly left behind, yet the penalty for murder is in a special class in the Bible. It was a universal statute before it was an Israelite one (Genesis 9:6). This point is weakened by being true also of the food law of Genesis 9:4. But the food laws were all repealed in the New Testament (*cf* 1 Corinthians 10:25, 27), whereas this was not, and then in Israelite law special reasons were given for allowing nothing to replace it (Numbers 35:31 *ff*). While this is far from conclusive, it makes one hesitate to argue from the disappearance of other institutions to the abolition of this one.

Secondly, the existence of such a penalty does not banish mercy or restraint. These can still be exercised. As a matter of history, nearly half the number of all convicted murderers in England and Wales in the first fifty years of this century were reprieved from execution (see the *Royal Commission Report on Capital Punishment* (HMSO, 1953), p. 13, where a figure of 45.7% is mentioned).

Then, to argue that death for murder shows disregard for life, is as false as to say that imprisonment for kidnapping shows disregard for liberty. Rather, the mild sentence is the one which tends to cheapen the offence in the eyes of society, by the comparisons it invites with other crimes and punishments.

Finally, for deterrence, as for anything else, cause and effect are notoriously hard to prove conclusively, but no one denies the phenomenal growth of violent crime in this country since the abolition of the death penalty in 1965. The new practice of classifying homicide as manslaughter wherever possible (on the plea of diminished responsibility) confuses the statistics but cannot hide the facts.

We were assured that this explosion would not happen; we are now assured that it is a coincidence. I find this implausible, even when allowance has been made for contributory causes.

All in all, then, capital punishment is in my view certainly defensible, possibly dispensable in some societies, but eminently justified by scripture, reason and experience.

**Derek Kidner**

**Further reading**

'The Humanitarian Theory of Punishment' C. S. Lewis *Churchmen Speak* (Marcham Manor Press)

*Ethics* A. C. Ewing (Teach Yourself Books, English Universities Press)

*Hard Sayings* Derek Kidner (IVP)

*The Philosophy of Punishment* H. B. Acton (Macmillan)

# 21
# Should we be responsible for our environment?

The enormous increase of scientific knowledge in the past two to three hundred years has led to a general understanding of *how* the world works, and a corresponding decrease in the mysterious areas which our ancestors too often envisaged was the place for God. Plough Sunday, Harvest Festival and the like were occasions for homage to a Super-Farmer capable of withholding blessing from the unwary. As God became confined more and more to the gaps in our knowledge, theologians (both evangelical pietists and catholic mystics) were forced to explain his activities as almost wholly spiritual. A rediscovery of the biblical doctrine of creation and its implications for the relationship of God to the world has long been necessary. It became crucial with the growing awareness in recent years of pollution, over-population, and resource depletion.

## Man's dominion over nature
According to Genesis 1:28 God gave to the man he had created in his image dominion over other living creatures. This authority has been taken by many Christians down the ages as a mandate to use both the living and inorganic worlds as God's gift for exploitation. This in turn has attracted the accusation that our environmental problems are the direct consequence of Christian teaching. This is often a fair comment.

For example, the seventeenth-century Puritans regarded New England as their Promised Land – a sanctuary from their Egypt, a testing ground, and a meeting place with God. Since Eden was a garden, they assumed that the reduction of wilderness to garden (and, incidentally, the reduction of the savage inhabitants of the land to civilisation through the Gospel) was a proper Christian task. To them, wild country was basically immoral: the hostility of nature to man was obvious – in flood and drought, forest and desert. Any action taken to bring wilderness into cultivation or, by labour, to exploit natural resources, partook of the quality of virtue. It was in terms of this Puritan wilderness-to-garden ethic that the advance of the frontier westward across America took place.

A comparable British example was the improvement of the Scottish Highlands in the first half of the nineteenth century, involving the clearance of the inhabitants to the coast or the colonies. In almost all cases this was supported by the local ministers. To conquer and control nature in such circumstances was no more than obedience to God's original command.

## Stewardship

This interpretation of the creation ordinance is a classical example of taking scripture out of its context. Since man is made in God's image, this means that he (*ie* we) must exercise reliability and responsibility. (The facile understanding that man has God's image through the possession of head, hands, legs, etc. is ridiculous, *eg* John 4:24). Consequently the dominion exercised by man is not to be an anthropocentric plunder of God's gifts to him, but rather a responsible stewardship of God's own world.

Most of the Bible teaching about the environment is in the Old Testament, but on several occasions Christ confirmed our mandate to work with the natural world in the role of a manager or steward, responsible as it were to a non-executive director. For example, Jesus uses the analogy of an absentee landlord for God (*eg* Luke 12:42–48, 19:12–27, 20:9–18, etc.). In other places the New Testament pictures man in his relation to nature as a shepherd, a farm manager or a household steward.

We have a God-given role to care for natural resources on behalf of our Lord – a role which allows us to make use of the resources for our own needs, but does not permit us to destroy them since they are entrusted to us only for a limited period. Man with nature is like a library-user: entitled and expected to make the best use of the contents, but trusted to handle the books properly so that they are available to others.

## Spiritual duty

When we recognise that our treatment of our physical surroundings is linked to our spiritual obedience to God the Creator, the Old Testament pledges about the Promised Land yielding bountifully *if* the Israelites behaved themselves make sense (*eg* Leviticus 26:3–5, Isaiah 24:5). To modern ears the linking of agricultural yield to moral behaviour sounds odd; it is *only* when we appreciate that both biological and purposive causes make sense in God who holds them together (Colossians 1:17) that we appreciate this paradox. It was the Israelites' disobedience in failing to take possession of the whole of the Promised Land (Judges 1:27–33) that produced over-crowding and fighting, and led to havoc in the fragile ecosystem (*ie,* growing conditions) of the eastern Mediterranean lands.

Our response to the environment must not be to neglect it as neutral, nor to hallow it as divine, but to *use* it as part of our spiritual duty. Indeed only if we see the world about us as God's good world, will we be able to involve ourselves with environmental problems with a responsibility as urgent as, say, teaching or evangelism (*qv* Romans 8:20–22). We are agents for God's purposes on earth. We fail if we attempt to discharge ourselves through church activities or Christian involvement in the usual sense of that phrase; and we fail equally if we sentimentalise pigs and primroses. The Israelites were placed by God in the easily upset ecology of Palestine. Now that the world has filled with people, it has become almost as vulnerable ('a fragile space-ship'). No longer can we run away from environmental problems like our forebears, because there is nowhere to escape to: our only hope is to accept the charge laid upon us in the first chapter of the Bible.

**R. J. Berry**

**Further Reading**
*Ecology and Ethics* R. J. Berry (IVP)
*The Dominion of Man* J. Black (Edinburgh University Press)
*Can Man Survive?* H. Montefiore (Fontana)
*Man and Nature* ed H. Montefiore (Collins)
*Whose World?* A. N. Triton (IVP)

## 22
# What should Christians be doing about the plight of the Third World?

The Bible says 'It is God's gift to man that everyone should eat and drink' (Ecclesiastes 3:13), yet tonight half the people living in our world will go to bed hungry. And tomorrow 12,000 people will literally starve to death. That is the daily death total of people who die of hunger. Why, when for the first time in human history we have means to feed all mankind? I think President Kennedy put the answer in a sentence: 'We lack only the willingness to share.'

To start with, those neat little economic labels that split mankind into separate segments reflect in themselves our selfishness and greed. For instance, 25% of the world's population enjoy and exploit 75% of the world's wealth and natural resources. Meanwhile three-quarters of the world's population – the so-called Third World – eke out their existence on the remaining 25% of the world's wealth.

**A vast problem**
Now in considering the plight of the Third World there is a tendency to feel overwhelmed by the enormity of its problems. Bombarded by reports through the press, radio and television, there is a temptation to switch off or 'do an ostrich' in order to maintain our sanity. Perhaps we feel like Robert Louis Stevenson when he wrote:

> The world is so big and I am so small,
> I do not like it at all, at all.

But as Dr Schumacher, one of the world's leading economists, states,

'Small is beautiful.' In other words, the smaller the project or programme the more likely its success. And in the most under-developed regions of Africa, Asia and Latin America the Christian Church has proved this simple theory in setting up model agricultural units, public health programmes, trade training schools, etc. Together, national Christians, missions and Christian agencies such as my own, have seen this thesis in action; small is both beautiful and meaningful. It provides help for the present and offers hope for the future. And it helps people to help themselves, which, in the long run, is the most effective form of assistance that anyone can be given.

Nevertheless there are those who ask, 'But why do you bother? The needs are overwhelming and your resources are totally inadequate. It's just a drop in the ocean.' Maybe. But as it has been said, 'The ocean is made up of many drops.' Mother Theresa of Calcutta shares a similar sentiment with Malcolm Muggeridge in his book *Something Beautiful for God*: 'We ourselves feel that what we are doing is just a drop in the ocean. But if that drop was not in the ocean I think the ocean would be less because of that missing drop.' Besides, the fact that I can't do everything is no reason why I shouldn't do anything! So what am I as a Christian called to do?

**Awareness of need**

Firstly, I am called to be *aware* – to be aware of the needs of the world in which I live and to be aware of my responsibility in helping to meet some of those needs. 'It is the task of the Christian man and the Christian society,' says Michael Green in his book *Jesus Spells Freedom*, 'both to keep informed as to what is threatening the world and to press for truly human priorities to be kept uppermost in national and international policies.' This kind of awareness will govern the way I vote at elections, determine my life style, clarify my priorities and give me a more realistic sense of perspective. It could even give me a new sense of vocation and alter my whole direction in life.

In an all-out attempt to foster and increase this awareness most Christian agencies use a whole range of publications and educational aids. And anyone who wants to can always get a sample pack from my own information department by writing to TEAR Fund's Information Officer, 1 Bridgeman Road, Teddington, Middlesex.

**Caring**

Secondly, we are called to *care*. 'If a mother cares,' runs the soap powder commercial, 'it shows.' And if we as Christians care – it must show. 'Little children,' writes the Apostle John, 'let us stop just saying we love people, let us really love them and show it by our actions' (1 John 3:18, Living Bible). For some, this could possibly lead to personal service in the Third World. It's a salutary thought that you could be the answer to somebody's prayer for meeting a need that God wants to meet through you. Maybe God is waiting to express his love and care through you in Africa, Asia or Latin America.

I remember in Bangladesh one of our TEAR Fund supported nurses sitting at supper after a particularly harrowing day in the refugee camps. 'I wonder at times,' she said, 'if God really cares for the people that are there.' It was a question born out of watching relentless suffering and hardship. But with great presence of mind a senior missionary said quietly, 'Yes, he cares. And you are there because God cares.' And it could be that God may want you *there* as an expression of his care.

## Sharing

Thirdly, we are called to *share*. In the last chapter of the Epistle to the Hebrews, the writer encouraged his readers to offer up through Jesus 'a sacrifice of praise to God, that is, the fruit of lips that acknowledge his name' (13:15). But, as the old prayer puts it, this praise is not only to be declared with our lips; it must also be demonstrated in our lives. This inter-relation becomes self-evident in Hebrews 13 when the passage goes on to say, 'Do not neglect to do good and to *share* what you have, for such sacrifices are pleasing to God' (16).

Remember that incident early in the Gospels when the people came to John the Baptist with a desire to make amends. 'What are we to do then?' they asked, and you will recall the answer: 'Whoever has food must *share* it' (Luke 3:10, 11). If then as Christians we really care, it will be shown by the extent in which we are prepared to share with others what we ourselves so richly enjoy. For, as St John says, 'If anyone has the world's goods and sees his brother in need yet closes his heart against him, how does God's love abide in him?' (1 John 3:17).

## Prayer

Fourthly, I am called to bear part of the burden of prayer for the Third World. 'Art thou weak and heavy laden,' runs the old hymn, 'cumbered with a load of care?' in times of personal temptation and difficulties we rejoice at being able to follow the hymn writer's advice and 'take it to the Lord in prayer.' But we must learn to widen the scope of this petition if we are prayerfully to bear the burdens of the Third World. Each night after watching the news reports on American television I gather that Billy Graham and his wife switch off and bow in prayer to God for the places and people they have just been watching.

It's a good start. 'Pray much for others,' says St Paul, 'plead for God's mercy upon them; give thanks for all he is going to do for them' (1 Timothy 2:1, Living Bible). For a Christian, this is one of our highest callings and ultimately one of our most meaningful contributions in co-operating with God for meeting the needs in his world.

**George Hoffman**

**Further reading**
*What about the Third World?* Roy Billington (IVP)

# 23
# What is wrong with pornography?

*Are* there any moral questions, as opposed to moral certitudes. attending the subject of pornography? At first sight it would all seem so clear. By definition, lexicographical or legal, pornography expresses or suggests the obscene; and the 'obscene,' again by definition, is offensive to modesty or decency; so any moral questions which arise about pornography *once it has been identified as such* would seem of a different order from those which appear when we are trying to pinpoint whether certain writings or pictures can be categorised as pornographic.

Hence there are two clusters of moral questions about pornography. One cluster has to do with identifying it. The other has to do with the nature of the 'offence' to which, if present, it gives rise. The clusters are closely related, but the difference between them is as important as their similarity.

## What is pornography?
To take the first cluster of questions: how do we, indeed *can* we identify pornography? The problem here is that, even by dictionary definition, absolute and relative scales are both applicable. To be pornographic the writing or painting must suggest the obscene, and the obscene is offensive either 'to modesty or decency' or 'to the senses or mind,' or both. This is where the strongly subjective element in the whole discussion becomes so important. We must begin by facing the fact that as individuals we do have different levels of tolerance, whether it is to pain or pollution: that the air on which some thrive is

death to the consumptive: and that the same is true of moral pollution. Hence what affects the senses or mind of one *may not* affect the senses or mind of another. But there is a level of our pollution beyond which no known human being can survive; and so miners and soldiers have died.

Secular society is slowly discovering that laws which operate in the physical realm do operate similarly on other dimensions of living, and that the spirit of a man can be choked as surely as his body. Hence the obscenity laws society promulgates in its own defence. But there is no basis of agreement about where to put the safety limit: though we now have agreed measurements of sound levels destructive to humanity or environmental pollution levels inimical to well-being, society has not yet really agreed on a similar Plimsoll line indicating that which is dangerous to the senses or mind in the realm of the obscene.

The reason for this is perfectly clear. There is going to be little possibility of harmonising the relative measurements when there is no agreement about the absolute. To say of something that it offends 'modesty' or 'decency' is, today, to beg the question about whether such qualities either exist or should exist; and that in spite of the goodwill which may be felt, in a vague and spongy way, towards both. To be pornographic means in some way to damage or violate human value; and if the humanity concerned does not *of itself* recognise that it has been damaged or violated, that its modesty or decency has been assaulted, it is extremely tricky to prove to it the case. It is difficult to restore to a burglar's victim property which he swears he never lost in the first place!

It will be apparent from this that the identification of pornography has to do with one's view of the nature of man, and as such has a moral dimension shaped by what our understanding is of his origin and destiny. If we believe man is God's creation, shaped in his maker's image, created to share in the divine delight, then our understanding of his essential activities and functions will accord with this. Mind and senses, modesty and decency, would then be offended by anything which denied either the delight or the sacredness of the sexual relationship; anything which divorced it from the real situation of the person, so that it led him away from a God-directed reality into a state of fantasy; anything which perverted the sexual by rooting it in the sadistic or the masochistic instead of the giving and receiving of delight.

## Questions to be faced

So there are certain questions we must ask ourselves strictly if we suspect writing or painting of pornography. There are few better tests of either our honesty or our humility than the way we face the questions.

First, does this work suggest the creativity and self-giving which properly attends a sexual relationship, or does it deny them? Why does it do so? Is it because one's own notion of sexual freedom and dignity is too rigid and narrow, or because this expression of the sexual is debasing?

Secondly, does this work stimulate me to a sexual excitement which is not correlated with my circumstances, so that I am led to a fantasy life which denies my real situation? (This is not to deny the importance of fantasy in life but to assert the need for it *to be recognised for what it is*, rather than as a substitute-reality which becomes a pretence for the real thing.) More fundamentally, does it present a view which illuminates and deepens or denies the realities of the sexual relationship? Does it depend for its effect on glamorising and removing the mundane responsibility of the sexual, or at the other extreme, on its aberration, or on the abnormal?

Thirdly, does it present sexual relationship in terms of self-gratification and the 'using' of another, merging into abuse both of the other and of oneself? That is, are the roots of it presented implicitly or explicitly, as violence and hate rather than love?

It is surprising how hard it is to answer these questions entirely honestly. Obviously we are all hostages of our society to some extent and we have to face seriously the current claim that pornography can to some degree be therapeutic. It is at this point that the divergence between a Christian ethic and the current social ethic becomes most apparent. There are two questions here. First, how far any of us can so detach himself from the society in which he lives that his values are not completely modified by it. C. S. Lewis has said much on the way we become insensibly adjusted to the *mores* of our society, so that, unaware, our code of discrimination is changed. Secondly, there is the question of how far the Christian has any right, as a member of a minority group, to prescribe for society laws which relate to his faith, the foundations for which are to be found in the Christian view of man (Romans 1:18–32; Colossians 1:15–19; Ephesians 4:17–5:33).

There is no space here to expand on an approach to these questions, beyond two essential points. In relation to the first, the

Christian is called to live in two worlds throughout his life, in the society of his day and in the community of the body of Christ. If he fully lives in both then there is an inbuilt system of counter-balance which will prevent him from ever becoming wholly assimilated to what Traherne has called 'the dirty devices of the world,' while he yet remains sensitive to what society may have to teach him (which last in its check on false pieties, pharisaical smugness, lack of insight, and self-generated sectarian views, can be very valuable). In relation to the second issue, since the Christian is declaring not what he thinks to be good only for Christians, but what he feels to be a fundamental truth about the creature man, the claim that Christians should not apply their views beyond their own minority group is irrelevant, just as environmentalists are concerned with what affects man whether he admits it or not, so are Christians, and there is nothing overbearing about their saying so.

## A sick society

This leads us into the second cluster of questions, those arising from the nature of the 'offence' to which pornography, once identified, gives rise. For the gap between what the Christian will identify as pornography and what his society may so define says something about the society itself. Here the close relationship between the two clusters of questions becomes obvious, and also the difference. The first cluster had at its centre what the Christian view is of man. The second cluster retains that view, but goes on to put at the centre of the question what it is that reveals itself by the presence of pornography. For the truth is that pornography itself is a symptom, not a disease: it is a significant eruption by which the nature and extent of a society's ill can be diagnosed. Where it exists to any significant extent it indicates a society which regards people as objects, not as beings of infinite worth; which has lost the capacity of reverence towards its individual members as creatures of dignity and sacredness; which is tormented and rends itself in violence, hatred and self-abuse; and which abandons responsibility in the context of realities for a dream of power and achievement in a fantasy world.

The questions which arise here are twofold. What should our attitude be towards a society so revealed? And secondly, What can or ought to be done about it? Again space allows for only the briefest approach. Concerning the question of the Christian's attitude, the key to his proper understanding must be that he is himself a member of the society he so diagnoses, and must stand under his own judgement. The self-righteous, minatory, merely accusatory, denies the truth of this, and was never a posture Christ himself adopted. Rather he came to the sick and searched out the cause of the sickness. Such 'searching' does not indulge the sickness but is astringent, does not compound with, but removes the root of, the disease.

It is important that Christians should be prepared to confess to themselves, as well as publicly, those ills of which as members of society they stand convicted. There can be no gap between public and private here. It is a measure of our society's 'double-think' that it can urge such a distinction and suggest that what is experienced in private is not a matter of concern for anyone else, that only the public pornography is of importance. As John Donne said, 'Any man's death diminishes me,' whether it be physical, moral or spiritual. So the distinction between public and private stances seems to be a non-question, nor can one make the issue one of 'harm' to others only, since by definition pornography *is* harmful.

## What is to be done?

This brings us to the final question, which can only be broached *after* we have looked at all the foregoing. This last question is the one usually raised first; hence the ambiguities and misunderstandings that arise. The concluding question must be, What is to be done about pornography? And here there is properly a twofold approach, one private and the other public. The private approach involves a humble and honest self-scrutiny which tests both one's own self-righteousness and one's own self-indulgence in the context of one's living relationship with God and one's fellow man, and adjusts one's practice accordingly. The public approach will require so positive an expression of the real glory of the human being's proper state that the way pornography represents him will be seen by comparison as diminishing and derogatory. Such an expression is to be made not only in words but in deeds and relationships, and its quality is essentially joyous, not denunciatory. It is true that nothing so dispels the effect of pornography as laughter. But there are different kinds of laughter, and that which most quickly not only heals the offence but also creates new life is the joyful laughter of the human being who delights in his Creator and in all things he has made.

**Ruth Etchells**

# 24
# Is violence ever justified?

The Christian is called to love his neighbour. This love is to be expressed in a deep concern both for man's spiritual needs and also for his material needs in everyday life. The difficulty lies in keeping these two aspects of ministry in balance together. Evangelical Christians have sometimes tended so to emphasise the evangelistic call that the social side of the Gospel has been underplayed. Over the past decades the World Council of Churches has moved strongly in the other direction. At first this was expressed in a concern for social aid, but it was increasingly realised that poverty and material needs were often due to political structures which perpetuated injustice. Changing these political or social structures became therefore the new dimension in Christian ministry.

Men of influence and wealth prefer to maintain the status quo. Violence seemed to be the only effective way to change existing political systems of oppression in the search for equality and justice. So the WCC supports revolutionary movements in Africa, and leading Churchmen may be involved in violent Marxist activity in Latin America.

'Violence of some sort is inevitable,' they say. 'Imperialism, economic oppression and social injustice are types of violence which lead to imprisonment, starvation and death.' Is overt revolution perhaps a lesser form which may introduce a new society of justice and righteousness? This would be the view of many today, including the exponents of Black Theology and the Theology of Liberation. Others maintain that violence always breeds more violence, and bitterness can never be the harbinger of love.

As biblical Christians we need to ask ourselves whether violence can be countenanced by Scripture. Mere philosophical or pragmatic answers cannot suffice.

## Old Testament teaching

*The historical books*

A strong emphasis on justice in everyday social dealings marked the life of Israel. Jehovah concerned himself deeply with details of life such as the right use of landmarks. Widows, orphans, aliens and the weak generally were to be protected through an incorrupt judiciary. So Exodus describes Moses acting as judge over Israel. Then in chapter 18 he establishes a more effective system. This chapter teaches three basic concepts:

 **i** God is the supreme judge over his people – and the Laws are his.
 **ii** God's appointed leaders are to teach his ways of justice and administer them.
 **iii** Corruption in the judiciary is utterly abhorrent to God.

In Deuteronomy 17 we find similar teaching with regard to the establishment of the monarchy. God allows Israel to have a king over them; he does not insist on a democratic form of government. But Israel's king is to have certain characteristics:

 **i** He is to be God's choice (17:15) and subject to God's law (17:18, 19).
 **ii** He must be humble because he is one with his people (17:15, 20).
 **iii** He will not trust in material wealth and power (17:16, 17).
 **iv** He is to be morally upright (17:17).

But this chapter gives no hint how Israel should deal with a bad king. The tacit assumption is that *God* will remove him (17:20). Even the parallel passage in 1 Samuel 8 also teaches that it is *God* who chose kings. The people can only 'cry out' if a king is evil; but still God does not necessarily answer their cry because of their sin.

The historical books do however reveal a God who is often violent and who sometimes commands his people to display violence. After the deliverance of Israel from Egypt Jehovah is called 'a man of war' (Exodus 15:3). The destruction of the Canaanite races by Israel at God's command is also hardly pacific! The old Hebrew Rabbis explained this (Mechilta 38b) by saying that 'it is only for the love of Israel that God appears in such a capacity.' Others say that bloodshed is only for the destruction of specific corrupt peoples in order to keep Israel from compromising relationships. God was teaching Israel the meaning of holiness.

We cannot however avoid the fact that Jehovah and his people killed and destroyed.

*The Prophets*

So from the beginning of Israel's history, violence is common and the early prophets also do not avoid words which encourage such action, but they themselves do not indulge in the shedding of blood – *eg* Ahijah in 1 Kings 11 and Elisha in 1 Kings 19. The writing prophets however do not even incite to violent action. They merely preach impassioned demands for justice and righteousness, denouncing leaders who betray their high calling. The prophets are not activist revolutionaries. They believe in a God who controls history and will in due time establish his kingdom of justice.

## The New Testament

Professor Brandon has tried to show that Jesus was a zealot revolutionary. Yoder, Hengel and others have shown this idea to be biblically indefensible. Jesus did not take up arms, nor did he incite his disciples to join the rebels. He refused to be made a human king, insisting that his kingdom was not of this world. Finally he submitted silently to his judges and executioners, like a sheep before its shearers. Willingly and without resistance he suffered and died.

Many Christians today are calling the Church to resume a prophetic ministry in fearless preaching against all oppression by right-wing or left-wing regimes. Verkuyl also encourages Christians to use non-violent weapons such as strikes. But the prophet who is not prepared to resort to the ultimate extreme of violence will be rejected by both wings of political opinion. He will also be condemned by the revolutionary as being too passive and therefore favouring the status quo. Non-violent prophetic preaching will be rejected, and can only lead to the Cross. Jesus too was rejected by zealots as being too passive, while the Romans crucified him as a political threat. The servant cannot be greater than his master.

However, the teachings of Jesus undermined the authoritarian claims of the Romans. Thus for example Roman coins had upon them the image of the emperor and could therefore be given to him in taxation. Man on the other hand is made in the image of God and can only be subject to God.

In Luke 3, John the Baptist attacked inequality, greed, and the wrong use of power. Jesus too in his miracles and in his teaching demonstrated his support for the weak and despised in society. He did not hesitate to criticise the leaders of political and religious life. In his aggressive ethic of love, Jesus boldly attacked anything that savoured of injustice and hypocrisy. His words and deeds were socially revolutionary; but violence was not his chosen means to usher in the revolution.

The apostles were accused of turning the world upside down. They caused disturbances in place after place by their words. The revolutionary power however was supplied by the Holy Spirit who was present in their prayer and preaching. They did not use force. They taught that as far as possible Christians should live peaceably with all (Romans 12:18).

The book of Revelation shows God in violent actions of judgement and to a lesser degree we see this same divine violence in other parts of the New Testament. Its teaching is consistent with that of the Old Testament: such violence is the province of God and not of man. Man preaches and teaches the demands of God for justice and righteousness; but such zeal must also be tempered with patient realism which recognises that the characteristics of the perfect kingdom of God cannot in this age be fully realised. On the other hand we are not to sit back idly and bemoan the world's slide into increasing evil as the climax of Christ's second coming approaches. God's passion for righteousness and for social justice is to enflame our hearts and drive us to loving action in word and deed. Nevertheless violence remains the activity of God in judgement.

**Martin E. Goldsmith**

**Further reading**
*The Politics of Jesus* J. H. Yoder (Eerdmans)
*Responsible Revolution* J. Verkuyl and H. G. S. Nordholt (Eerdmans)
*The Political Christ* A. Richardson (SCM)
*Victory over Violence* M. Hengel (SPCK)
*Revolutionary Theology Comes of Age* J. M. Bonino (SPCK)
*Violence – Right or Wrong?* P. Macky (Word Books)

# 25
# Should a Christian use drugs?

Whenever the subject of drug use is mentioned there is a tendency first of all for us to think of some type of young person's problem involving the taking of illicit drugs. The issue for the Christian is much broader than this.

## How do drugs act?
As far as we can tell mankind has been using drugs since earliest times, finding potions to heal the body, kill disease or change the state of the mind. Our society has developed its chemical technology considerably and we are able to benefit from all manner of drugs which both ease pain and combat disease. If we compare our life with conditions of a century ago we can see the tremendous benefits that drugs have brought to society today. At the same time we have to be aware of the fact that we seem to be less able to deal with stress and anxiety and some drugs are an easy and effective way of blotting out reality, if only temporarily.

By far the majority of drugs act as selective poisons. They do not produce miraculous reactions by adding something to the body. Instead, they kill off something which has entered the system or else poison the activity of one part of the body in such a way as to aid the remainder of it. If they are used indiscriminately they can cause short or long term problems or dependence (once called addiction).

## Where do drugs fit into society?
In Britain, we control most drugs so that only doctors can prescribe

them. A doctor is able to decide the correct dose, the period of time for which the chemical can be given, and possible side effects. This system is open to abuse where a patient pressurises the doctor for drugs for conditions which could be treated in other ways.

Another group of drugs which can be prescribed by doctors, together with some substances with no medical use, are controlled under the *1971 Drug Misuse Act*. These drugs are sold illicitly by various people who are either addicted themselves or who make a profit from the sale of drugs. Because of the damage they can cause to the individual, and the ability of people to pressurise others to use them, possession of and trading in these drugs and their use are punishable by fine or imprisonment. In this group are various sedatives and stimulants, narcotics (drugs derived from, or similar to opium) and substances which change the functioning of the mind like the hallucinogens (LSD) and cannabis (pot).

A third group of drugs could be described as store drugs. These are the countless substances sold over the counter for every conceivable minor ailment. Some can be very useful, like aspirin, but others are of more dubious worth, and during the last decade there has been a sharp increase in the availability and sale of such substances. There has been a growth too in the number of people who now *take something* for the slightest ache or pain.

Yet another group of drugs consists of those classed as socially acceptable. In Britain, caffeine which is found in tea and coffee, does little harm unless people take excessive doses. However another acceptable drug, nicotine, is considered responsible for the deaths of 50,000 to 80,000 people every year. Alcohol does not kill people in the same numbers or the same way but is responsible for large numbers of road accidents and is acknowledged as a major causative factor in the levels of crime, violence etc. in modern life. We have developed a society where few people are objective about their own drinking habits and where we have about half a million alcoholics.

## The guiding principles controlling use and abuse

If we consider any drug that we are going to use, the circumstances we are using it in and the reason for use we should think carefully about the following:

*What are its immediate effects?*
Will it affect the way my mind or body functions and make me any

the less able to respond to doing God's will or make me more prone to damaging myself or others? As Christians we see our minds and bodies as gifts from God, to be used for him, and at any time available for his use.

*Is it possible that a habit may build up by the use of this drug?*
If so could that harm my body or mind in the future? (1 Corinthians 3:16–18; 1 Corinthians 6:19; 2 Corinthians 6:16).

*Will it make me behave any differently from normal?*
As Christians we are called to be in control of all of our faculties. (Romans 6:13; 2 Peter 3:17).

*Could this drug, in the way I am using it, cause addiction?*
Addiction takes away all self control. Behaviour of this sort is in complete opposition to the Christian's understanding of conduct. (Proverbs 20:1; Isaiah 5:11; Luke 21:34).

*Am I respecting the opinions of others?*
By taking a drug in a particular setting you may inconvenience others or make it difficult for others to stick to their principles.

*What example am I setting to others?*
We need to be conscious of the fact that even if we believe we are able to be responsible in our use of one type of drug, another person following our example may be totally unable to control its use. (Romans 14 especially vv. 10, 13, 14, 19, 21. See also the table at the end of this article).

## What is the Christian response to drugs in society?

First, we have to recognise that we are living in God's world, and his scheme of things includes the beneficial use of drugs. Many of the scientists who discovered drugs were Christians. We are abusing God's gifts just as much if we take the 'head in sand' attitude of 'I'm not taking anything at all.'

Secondly, we need to plan how we are going to take drugs. We each need our own pattern. Are we going to take drugs just when they are prescribed? Are we going to drink or smoke? If so, what controls are we going to put over our drug taking?

Thirdly, and most important, we need to think about situations in

| Drug | Any short term problem? | Any long term problem? |
|---|---|---|
| Prescribed drugs | Normally the doctor will warn if there is any danger: *eg* if there are foods which should not be eaten with the drug. | The doctor is able to decide when to stop the course to prevent long term problems. |
| Store drugs | Warnings on labels: *eg* do not drive whilst using drug. If heeded, no problems. | Some people take so many that they slowly poison the body. |
| Tobacco Nicotine | Inconvenience to others. | Causes considerable predisposition to lung cancer, other cancers, bronchitis, thrombosis. In majority of smokers will shorten life span and impair body reactions and health after period of time. |
| Alcohol | It slows down the brain after taking. Person therefore more prone to road accidents or other accidents. Person loses inhibitions, also becomes over-confident. Tendency for people to relax their limits once affected by alcohol. Affects brain for considerable time (one pint for three hours though this does vary). Heavy dose can cause sleep or death. | Excessive regular use damages organs particularly stomach and liver. |
| *Illicit drugs* Barbiturates | Slow brain, easy to take overdose, make the user more prone to accidents. | Easy to become addicted by long term use. Tendency to increase dose. |
| Stimulants | Side effect of tensions and exhaustion. Easy progression to regular use. | Strong psychological (mind) dependence. |
| Hallucinogens (LSD) | The taker does not know what he is doing or what is really happening around him. | Can cause mental disorientation or occasionally physical harm by inducing accidents. Can bring out latent mental problems. |
| Cannabis | Slows down brain. Makes person very subjective to experience accidents if driving. | Psychological dependence. Brings out latent problems in some. |
| Narcotics | Slows brain. Easy for overdose. | Numerous physical complications. Overdoses easy. |

| *Will it change behaviour?* | *Will it cause addiction?* |
|---|---|
| If a particular drug is going to make a person depressed or moody the doctor will normally warn about this. | The doctor knows when to stop the drug to prevent this. Only if the patient pressurises for some types of drugs can this occur. |
| If used in large quantities and poisoning occurs then irrational behaviour may result. | If a person uses them automatically rather than for specific ailments (carefully obeying instructions) psychological addiction can occur. |
| If a person tries to give up smoking, he may find it hard or else become tense when he cannot smoke. | Some people are addicted to the nicotine in tobacco and cannot stop smoking. |
| Alcohol prevents clear thinking. In some people it will make them perform acts they would not normally commit. A considerable amount of crime, violence, wife and child-beating and neglect is precipitated by alcohol. As the brain is slowed down, there is no way to be certain alcohol will not change behaviour. | Alcoholism. (Very few are down and outs). Two danger signs are people drinking excessively or people drinking to alleviate tensions, bolster themselves up or deal with stress. |
| Person starts to rely on drug. | Strongly addictive. |
| The user becomes progressively drug orientated. | Strongly addictive. |
| The user becomes very subjective in viewing drug experience. Sometimes he loses touch with reality. | The experience becomes addictive. |
| Those who use this become introspective. | Psychological dependence can occur. |
| The user becomes totally drug orientated. | Strongly addictive. |

With illicit drugs a further complication is that there is no complete control over what the substance is, its purity, dosage or effects on any individual.

which we may find ourselves, where we will be asked to modify our drug taking. For instance, if you decide not to drink, how will you react at the party when only alcohol is available? Or, if you set a certain limit on the amount you drink, how do you react to the friend who pressurises you to drink more than your limit? Then suppose you decide a Christian cannot take illicit drugs; how will you react when you find yourself at a party where cannabis is being passed around? Again, you might feel tense (and it is quite respectable for Christians to feel like this!). Will you take a tranquilliser or how else will you react?

Finally, the Christian has a tremendous contribution to make to society in helping those affected by drugs. Working with drug addicts is not glamorous, contrary to the picture put around at times. It is an extremely hard field, but one in which practical help can be given. The contact with a person affected by drugs is of great importance in aiding him to gain a concept of himself as a person who matters to God, and who can be cured from his dependency by experiencing the deepest healing of personality which is to be found only in Christ. Any Christian church or group can seek to support people with chemically orientated problems and become a loving caring community where the outcasts feel they belong. We must never give glib answers to their problems, or when they slip back, but must accept them as they are, as people suffering from a severe illness. If they slip back again and again, we need to remember that this does not mean they are any the less Christian. It just means that we as Christians are not caring enough to give them the support to persevere.

**James Cowley**

**Further reading**
*The Abuse of Drugs* D. Pott and D. Vere (IVP)
*The Alcoholic and the Help he Needs* M. M. Glatt (Priory Press)
*Drugs in Modern Society* N. Imlah

# 26
# Isn't censorship out of date in a free, democratic society?

Censorship is an emotive word. A censor originally meant quite simply a person who reckons or estimates the value of something. But now primarily censorship has come to be used of the control of human communications. It is particularly applied to the control of what may be said in public, published in printed form, or represented pictorially or upon a stage. Since one of the fundamental values of Western democracy is that of freedom of speech, the idea of any sort of official control of the spoken or written word, or of what is visually conveyed by pictures or acting, naturally starts with the presumption that it is to be deplored.

## The good of society
However, even in the most civilised and democratic societies certain restraints upon communications have always been accepted as being for the wider good of that society. Thus in our own country what may be said or printed about other people is subject to the law of libel. What may be discussed publicly about certain aspects of Government policy and of Britain's defences in the event of war is subject to the Official Secrets Act. The inviolability of legal proceedings once they have been commenced is protected by the law of contempt. Blasphemy is restrained by certain legal sanctions.

The Christian view of human nature, while sympathising with the presumption in favour of freedom as a useful starting-point, will never forget that man is by nature sinful, and has tremendous potential for exploiting his neighbour. Hatred, aggression and corruption are in his heart from birth as well as the instinct to seek nobler things. It is therefore both realistic and biblical to watch for those types of communication which are peculiarly harmful and infectious, and to restrain them in any age. How much official control is needed will vary according to the moral quality of the cultural context.

It is now time to look in a little more detail at the various types of control which might be included under the heading of censorship. Professor Peter G. Richards in *Parliament and Conscience* (Allen & Unwin) provides a useful four-fold analysis:

Censorship may be formal or informal; it may be prospective or retroactive. Formal censorship depends on rules of conduct imposed by authority while informal regulation stems from social taboos. Prospective censorship operates on material before it is publicly available so that the censor's decision may not become public knowledge, while retroactive censorship suppresses matter already published. Pre-publication control is more effective and convenient for a censor because the alternative invites widespread comment on his decisions.

## Retroactive censorship
*Formal and informal*

Following the four-fold division given above, let us first consider retroactive censorship – *ie*, that which affects a publication's status after it has appeared and been made available. *Formal retroactive censorship* is simply a matter of law. The rules are existing legislation and those who apply them are the courts. A man publishes but at his own risk. If his publication is unlawful, it is suppressed in the sense that he is punished and the offending article whether statements or pictorial matter no longer circulates. In a democracy these decisions are only taken after a public procedure which ensures that competent people determine whether or not the law has been broken.

*Informal retroactive censorship* signifies some kind of tacit agreement that certain things shall not be accessible to the public even though the law does not prohibit them and there are those willing to make them available. Such a reaction is exemplified by people in the distribution chains through which articles are conveyed to the public, such as film distributors and exhibitors, and the newsagents' distribution chain. The decision not to stock or to distribute a book or a film can effectively secure its suppression.

## Prospective censorship

Prospective censorship, sometimes called pre-censorship, is the usual area denoted by the word. Here we have a peculiarly powerful means of control over information, attitudes and values, especially in an age of mass media communications.

*Informal prospective censorship* has been and still is typified by the activities of the broadcasting media. Within radio and television, in both the commercial and the public service bureaucracies, individual men and women are invested with great power of informal control over broadcast material. This has always been so, but it is a fact of life which many in our society have not yet faced. In the days when Lord Reith was Governor-General of the BBC this control was largely exercised in such a manner as to respect what might be loosely called Christian moral standards. Material challenging such standards or offensive to them was not broadcast by the tacit agreement of all the personnel involved. In the same way such censorship (if we may so call it) is now exercised in precisely the reverse direction, so that strongly Christian statements and viewpoints are rarely expressed, and some radio and TV broadcasts *already recorded* are never transmitted because of their clear moral stance. This informal pre-censorship applies also to certain organisations representing particular viewpoints, who cannot get articles or letters into the correspondence columns of certain newspapers; and when the commercial interests which support the Independent Broadcasting Authority channels are also those who have large or controlling holdings in mass circulation newspapers, the possibilities for censorship are even more sinister.

Informal prospective censorship can be seen therefore as something which may from a Christian point of view be good or bad. When it is exercised in the sphere of morals to keep the tone of public discussion responsible, sensitive and respectful of human dignity, then offensive and degrading material will rarely appear by tacit consent. However in the sphere of political discussion and information it is vital that there should be adequate treatment of all viewpoints and possibilities, and in particular that no commercial interests should wield power over communications which they may exercise to the moral detriment of the community, or in such a way as to close debate on complex political issues. Thus we conclude that Christians will be very sensitive to commercial or political manipulation through informal prospective censorship, but grateful for those informal arrangements which exert a controlling *moral* filter in this area.

Our final variety of censorship is *formal prospective censorship*. This is the most precise usage of the word and probably the one for which it should be retained. In this sense we speak of a closed body (however appointed) which screens or sifts material according to known criteria before such material may be publicly communicated.

Formal prospective censorship is widely used in totalitarian countries where any information likely to raise doubts in the minds of the public about the wisdom of the policies adopted by the dictator or the only political party permitted to exist is not granted public expression. Because of its close association with tyrannical forms of government, formal prospective censorship is deplored, and usually rightly so.

## Film censorship

An early screening process by a responsible public body is not always a bad thing, even in a democratic society. The main requirement must surely be that the powers of such a body must be clear and its criteria and decisions open to public scrutiny. Properly applied, such powers can save those wishing to publish offensive material from the risk of prosecution and from wasting resources on a particular enterprise by consulting the censorship body beforehand.

The British Board of Film Censors in this country is not a statutory body and its certificates have no legal value. The fact that it has refused to grant a certificate to a film cannot prevent its exhibition. Local authorities possess powers by which they can refuse to permit the showing of any film, or they can alter the classification of any film from that on the certificate which the Board has awarded. Few local authorities welcome the task of maintaining a viewing committee which regularly previews questionable films on behalf of local community standards, but in response to public protest many have rightly come to accept this as part of their duty on behalf of the health of the community. They deserve the sympathy and support of all Christian citizens.

Where public taste is good, pure and strong, there is little need of censorship and even the law will not be needed often. But where the moral consensus is weak, where perverted individuals and commercial interests are heedless of social damage, or even trying to wreck society and its fundamental institutions such as the family, a strong law at least will be needed, and perhaps even pre-censorship too. Montesquieu said 'Where religion is strong the law can be weak, but where religion is weak the law must be strong.'

**O. R. Johnston**

**Further reading**
*The Media* David Porter (Scripture Union)
*A Better Way* Frederick Catherwood (IVP)
*Pornography and Hate* David Holbrook (The Responsible Society)

# 27
# Should we advertise?

For the life of me I cannot understand why advertising requires an apologia any more than the motor trade, the furniture industry, the rag trade and a host of others. No one is going to suggest that the motor trade has no rogues, that all furniture manufacturers produce high quality merchandise or that some clothing is not rubbish; and he would be a fool who even hoped that the methods of all advertisers could possibly be beyond reproach. There are good and bad Christians, but that does not mean the faith is suspect.

Now I am aware that there is a vocal minority holding the theory that in a correctly ordered state advertising in unnecessary. Yet despite its objections to the competitive economy, the USSR has introduced advertising because without it there was little incentive to raise product standards. The big mistake of the idealist is to forget that human nature is not 'ideal,' and competition is essential and healthy for the human animal.

## Advertising is communication
Advertising assumes there is something to be communicated, whether in the promotion of ideas, persons or merchandise. It comes to us through posters, brochures, magazines, newspapers, cinema screen, TV and radio, salesmen at our doors, the church notice board, and the notices in church. All have something to say or sell. The first question must be, 'What is being promoted?' and the second, 'Should it be promoted at all?' This immediately takes the responsibility away from the advertising profession and places it squarely on the manufacturer. But who is going to be responsible for saying what is or is not to be produced? The total abstainer would say,

'Ban all alcohol,' the non-smoker would feel the same about tobacco. Some folk would like to see all cars off the road etc., etc. Who is to decide?

Any activity – whether it be social, cultural, religious or economic – within a human society is bound to be tainted with the sinfulness of those involved. Advertising is no exception. While it does not create the standards, it does mirror those already prevalent within society.

Therefore I maintain if it is right to produce a product, then it is right to advertise it.

## Advertising and society

The inventor invents, the manufacturer takes the invention and with modern technology produces it for the mass market, advertisements tell the public about the product and mass purchasing keeps the wheels of industry turning smoothly. If the inventor alone continued to produce small numbers of the product, the limited supply would make the unit cost phenomenal and the article would be available only to the rich, but the streamlining of factory production lines makes the product available to the mass market at a price it can afford. This is not producing more materialism, it is merely making that which already exists available to more people. We have left behind the philosophy which says,

> The rich man in his castle,
> The poor man at his gate,
> God made them high and lowly,
> And ordered their estate.

It has been argued that if the high cost of advertising was removed from the price of the product, merchandise would be cheaper; yet without advertising the consumer would never know about the product, and small demand would put us back to square one with a high-priced, under-consumed commodity. Around 1970, advertising expenditure in Britain was about £6000 million, yet this represented only $1\frac{1}{2}\%$ of total consumer spending. Mass markets require mass production and factories, and these must have workers, and workers rely on work for their own good standard of living. Advertising is vital to full employment in Britain.

Let us go back to that other point about *advertising creating needs*. No manufacturer would go into production without first testing the market. Research teams descend on a selected area where they expose the proposed product to the potential customers. Not until they are satisfied that an enthusiastic market exists and that the product is modified to conform to the requirements of that market, do they go into production. The need is already there and the advertisers discover that need.

Of course there are many similar products making claims to consumer benefits which often sound extravagant. Variety provides us with a choice, and freedom of choice has always been a strong point in Britain. But much more than this, it saves the consumer from being exploited. Manufacturers are constantly analysing their competitors' products and trying to out-do each other. In this way the *product is exploited, not the housewife*, because she gets the benefit in improved products, and lower prices.

## Bending or stretching the truth?

It is absolutely essential that we retain our sense of humour where advertisements are concerned. There's little enough in life these days to make people laugh, so why not take the advertisements less seriously and enjoy them. Many do little more than leave us with a happy association with the subject. No one believes for a minute that the clear, cool Heineken 'reaches the parts other beers cannot reach' thereby making the tired feet of policemen wriggle, and the sparse foliage on the old dame's fancy hat develop into a veritable Chelsea Flower Show! We need to remember that much of the content of the advertisement is to gain our attention and make the product stay in our minds. And since we are going to buy one of the products anyway, good luck to the advertiser who creates the right atmosphere for his product. There are many folk like me who laugh with the advertisement but are not sold by it – we just do not like lager.

Critics will say that some statements are made which are either misleading or down-right dishonest, making doubtful promises and offering misleading benefits to purchasers. Yes, it does sometimes happen, but any section of society is only as good as the people who compose it or else there would be no need for rules, but it would be quite wrong to say that all advertisements are misleading. The Advertising Standards Authority has a comprehensive set of regulations which state that all advertising should be legal, decent, honest and truthful, and that the code is to be applied not only in the letter, but in the spirit. Anyone suspecting an advertiser of making a dishonest claim can institute proceedings against the offender for violating the Trade Descriptions Act. The Independent Broadcasting Authority exercise a truth control on advertisements. Very few advertisers will risk their future and goodwill by going against this British Code of Advertising Practice. Also, if advertisers indulge in dishonest methods of advertising and complaint is made to the NPA the newspaper or magazine concerned may refuse to accept further space booking from the advertising agency which placed the advertisement, and that could put an agency out of business overnight. It just is not worth the risk.

## The hidden persuaders

It has been suggested that advertising plays on people's fears, hopes and insecurities as a means to sell products; and it is only a short step from this to say that human nature is exploited to make money. Here I believe we are playing with words. Does someone else always have to be blamed because I am human, have certain desires and attempt to fulfil them? Is it wrong to want to be warm in winter, have a comfortable home, and provide the best food and opportunities for my children? It is also felt that the alleged powerful techniques of persuasion used are dangerous because they play on our basic human nature, particularly where sex is concerned. Some advertisers do go too far in what they portray, yet nothing like as far as the rest of the media to which the buying public is exposed. The subcommittee of Lord Longford's committee dealing with advertising were satisfied that there was little evidence of pornographic appeal being used in advertising. Of course there are sometimes isolated spots of bad taste, but it would be unfair to claim that all advertising is so unhealthy.

Advertising does not function in a vacuum. The strange thing is that critics never see *themselves* as threatened by the techniques; rather they claim to be protecting someone else. The 'attention getter' may make us look at the product and we may even buy it, but if the product is not what we want, we will not buy it a second time. It is not unusual to hear the expression 'subliminal advertising' used in connection with sales promotion. This kind of advertising is highly specialised, quite immoral, and comes pretty close to brain-washing, but happily is forbidden by law to be used in Britain.

## Christian standards

It is ridiculous for Christians to think they can impose their biblical standards on the advertising profession, any more than any other industry. But the Christian does have a role to play and a responsibility to exercise in that part of the industry with which he or she is involved. It is wise to remember that while good laws are made, they are only so made because man is sinful and without them our society would be in anarchy. There are many secular rules controlling advertising practise, and these must be upheld.

The Bible teaches 'Provide things honest in the sight of all men,' 'Shun the appearance of evil' and the *Christian advertiser* will take extra care to make sure this is carried out in his work. He will remember his weaker brother and this may mean that he will decline to handle certain products which violate his Christian conscience. There are many things which our society and culture permit which a Christian may have to think twice about in the light of Christ's teaching. We all have a responsibility to clean up our society where necessary. Christians have an added responsibility. The advertising profession is responsive to public opinion, and if Christians devoted more of their energies to awakening public opinion, this could achieve far more success than constantly complaining about the profession itself.

**Alan J. Wagstaff**

# 28

# With millions of people living and dying in the world, can God really care about the individual?

There are really two questions here. There is the one on the surface, and there is the question beneath the question. The former asks whether God *can* care. And the answer 'Yes' can be given by the followers of most religions who believe in a personal God of some kind, and even by those of no religion who accept that the world that we live in is the work of a being outside itself. If we say that such a God is infinite, it means that he is not limited by anything outside himself. And if he is infinite, he can be infinitely great as well as infinitely small.

The God of the galaxies is also the God of the atom.

To say this is to give an intellectual answer to an intellectual problem. But beneath the surface question lies a deeper one. There is not only the problem of whether God can care, but whether he actually *does* care. Is God really concerned for the countless victims of atrocity and disaster that we calmly watch on our TV screens – and the millions more that we never see? To understand the Christian answer to this question we have got to look at it at long range and at short range. Looking at the question at long range, means asking what kind of a world is it that God has put us in. By looking at it at short range I imply asking what the Bible says about the care that God shows for us.

## What kind of a world?

What kind of a world is it that God has put us in? In a perfect machine nothing can go wrong. Every part has its place, and functions in the way that it is designed to. But it has no choice! It cannot respond on its own initiative. It has no say in the matter. It just functions. But the kind of world that God has put us in is not like that. God has paid man the intolerable compliment of handing over to him the choice of how he is to run his life. And with it he has created the possibility of making wrong and selfish choices.

Now this has bearing on the kind of care that God has for his creation. When the Bible talks about the love of God, nothing could be further from the 'smother love' that is always interfering. Real love is not giving the child everything that it wants on demand. The best gifts are those which enable the child to develop its faculties and grow as a person. And the best relationships are those which foster mutual response. But we cannot have it both ways. We cannot have a situation in which God has given real freedom and responsibility to man to live and grow in mutual love, and at the same time one in which God rushes in like an interfering grandmother whenever things go wrong.

Moreover, it is part of God's loving care that the laws of nature remain constant. The same fire that gives us warmth can also burn and destroy. The water that quenches thirst and is necessary to support life can also drown. We cannot expect God to bend the laws of nature every time we get in a jam. The kind of world that God has put us in is one in which we are able to use the things which belong to it for good or ill. In a church in which I once served we had a visiting card which said, 'The world is in a mess. But is it any wonder, if we neglect the maker's instructions?' Part of the maker's instructions is that we should love God with our whole being and our neighbours as ourselves (Matthew 22:37 *ff*; Mark 12:32 *ff*; Luke 10:27 *f*). Part of God's care is to give us the opportunity – and the obligation – to do just that.

## God's care

This brings us to what the Bible says about God's care for us. Its message is, in fact, double-edged. On the one hand, God cares in the sense that all men will have to give account to him. If we neglect the physical laws of the universe, we can hurt ourselves and bring misery to others. The same applies to its spiritual laws. The apostle Paul put it like this: 'Do not be deceived; God is not mocked, for whatever a man sows, that he will also reap' (Galatians 6:7). Elsewhere he reminded his readers that we shall all appear before the judgement seat of Christ (2 Corinthians 5:10; *cf* Romans 14:10; Philippians 2:10 *ff*). The same thought featured in the teaching of Jesus himself (Matthew 25:31–46). When someone pointed out a disaster which had befallen some people, thinking that it was a sign of God's judgement on them, Jesus replied, 'Unless you repent you will all likewise perish' (Luke 13:3, 5).

But God's care is not simply concerned with calling us to account. Just as the kind of world that God has put us in invites co-operation and trust between men, so the kind of relationship which God invites men to enter with him is one of co-operation and trust. He cares enough to send his Son that whoever believes in him should not perish but have eternal life (John 3:16). Paul wrote: 'We know that in everything God works for good with those who love him, who are called according to his purpose' (Romans 8:28). He went on to make it clear that this did not mean that we should be spared all pain and suffering. Indeed, it is sometimes just the opposite. For Paul went on to list tribulation, distress, persecution, famine, nakedness, peril and the sword. It is in and through these things – when men do their worst and seem to be in complete control – that God works and turns them into good with those who love him. In the same way Jesus spoke of the hairs of the disciple's head all being numbered and the sparrow not falling to the ground without the Father's will (Matthew 10:29 *f*; Luke 12:6 *f*). The experts on Jewish society in the first century tell us that the sparrows in question were not being sold as pets but to be killed as food for the poor. Even so, God is in control.

## A paradox

This is one of the great paradoxes of the Christian faith. On one level, man seems to be in control and all events happen according to the laws of nature. But at a deeper level God is working in these events for the good of those who love him and trust him.

Yet the paradox does not stop there. For the good for which God is working may not always appear good at first sight. Although we are spared some pain and suffering, we are not spared all. There are things which in the last analysis are more important than physical well-being. What God cares about most is the kind of people that we are, and God is caring most when sometimes he seems to be caring least.

**Colin Brown**

**Further reading**

*The Problem of Pain* C. S. Lewis (Fontana)
*Evil and the God of Love* John Hick (Fontana)
*The Christian Universe* E. L. Mascall (Darton, Longman & Todd)

# 29
# Should a Christian get mixed up in politics?

There are many Christians who believe most strongly that a Christian should not get mixed up in politics. They believe that politics is a dirty game and that Christians should have no part of it. Yet there are other Christians who feel exactly the opposite. They believe that Christians in responsible positions can do great good and that political power should not be allowed to be a monopoly of those who might abuse it. Which of these two positions is right?

## The powers that be
The Christian starts from the belief that, as Paul taught, 'the powers that be are ordained of God' (Romans 13:1). This was also taught by Peter (1 Peter 2:13–17), and by our Lord in his famous saying, 'Render to Caesar the things that are Caesar's, and to God the things that are God's' (Mark 12:17). In the context, the expression 'the powers that be' refers to government and the primary purpose of government is to maintain order, to restrain and punish evil and to reward good.

To do this, governments do not have to be perfect. Governments in the days of Christ and the apostles were imperial and arbitrary, not nationalist or democratic. Their governors were unjust and took bribes, and their tax collectors took more than their due. But the Christians were told by Christ and the apostles to obey them unless they interfered in matters of faith. If Christians were forbidden by government to preach the gospel or told to worship the emperor, then, of course, they disobeyed. As Peter said, 'We ought to obey God rather than men' (Acts 5:29).

In most countries in the world the Christian has about as much chance of becoming a part of government as Peter had of replacing Pontius Pilate or Paul had of replacing Festus or Felix. Their duty of obedience to lawful commands is the limit of the Christian involvement in politics. In countries where the ruling party is atheistic or committed to another religion, the Christian cannot be a member and is effectively excluded from politics and power. He may still, like Joseph or Daniel, act as an adviser, but he will not allow himself to be committed to the beliefs or shibboleths of the ruling party.

## Christian influence

Yet we have to remember that the influence of Christians outside politics can still be enormous. It was the Christian church which survived and not the Roman Empire, and Christian ideals which were gradually accepted through Europe rather than the ideals of the Romans. So even where Christians have no place in politics, they can by their ideals and example gradually change the political climate in which they live. We are taught to pray for rulers and those in authority. We are also taught to pray that God's will should be done on earth as it is in heaven. We should believe that God can answer the prayers he has taught us. But Christ also taught that 'whoever takes the sword shall perish with the sword' (Matthew 26:52). It is not only lack of faith but disobedience to attempt a violent overthrow of government, even a corrupt and arbitrary government like that of Imperial Rome.

In most countries where Christian influence has prevailed there are democratic governments and a Christian can stand as a candidate for election to local or national government. Many Christians feel that they have no right to impose Christian principles on those who are not Christians. They also feel that it would be wrong to compromise those principles for something else. So they feel that they cannot accept political responsibility. Their problem is that they do not distinguish between the moral law under which man answers to God and the civil law under which we answer to our fellow men.

## The moral law

When Christ said that divorce was contrary to God's will it was pointed out to him that Moses had allowed it – and who was he to contradict Moses? His answer was that Moses had allowed divorce for the hardness of their hearts, 'but from the beginning it was not so'

(Matthew 19:8). Moses was the civil order. He gave Israel the Ten Commandments, which embody the moral law. But he also gave laws of the land – rules for the people of Israel to be enforced by their rulers. If a man loves his wife as he loves himself, according to the moral law he will not divorce her. But hard-hearted men, though they cannot be persuaded to keep the moral law, still may be persuaded by the penalties of the civil law not to throw out their wife without going through a proper form of divorce in which the law will protect the wife's rights.

A Christian politician who passes bills allowing divorce does not deny his principles any more than Moses denied his. Both are doing their best in the circumstances. But a Christian politician can also try to persuade his fellow-citizens to raise their standards. Wilberforce and his friends abolished the slave trade. Shaftesbury and his friends prevented the abuse of child labour. Both groups acted as Christian politicians on Christian principles.

All countries need some ultimate moral standard. No country can survive for long unless there is a moral basis to its laws, a basis on which men can agree. Those who are not Christians try to make up their own moral basis. But why should anyone agree with them? They tell people not to be greedy and no one takes too much notice. It needs more than exhortation to turn back greed, to curb violence, to make the rich pay taxes to help the poor, to make the strong stand aside to help the weak. The Christian in politics can contribute his knowledge of a divinely revealed moral order which men are happier if they keep and which has been applied and tried in all kinds of societies for two thousand years.

But politics is also about power, and power, like money, can corrupt. The Christian in politics must not regard power as his supreme objective. In his attempts to be elected and to gain power for his party he must do nothing against the Christian standards of conduct. If he does, he will destroy his usefulness as a Christian. The saying 'If God be for us, who can be against us?' is not a guarantee that Christians will win elections without trying. But Christians have found that a reputation for honourable behaviour does not in the end hinder, and often helps them, to get elected.

**Frederick Catherwood**

**Further reading**
*A Better Way* Frederick Catherwood (IVP)

# 30
# How can a Christian have an impact on the local community?

On the Sunday afternoon before writing this article I was present with my wife at a meeting with Bengalis in their own house in our street. It was not until I was asked to say a few words that I recalled that our being there was not because I was rector of the parish, but because I was chairman of the Spitalfields Community Action Group (SCAG). The meeting had been convened by the Bengali Action Group, to meet SCAG socially. It was an epoch-making occasion, as their spokesman rightly said when replying. For at least fifteen years, more and more Asians have been coming into Spitalfields until now they make up probably two-thirds of the immediate population. Our church day school is 85% immigrant and 75% of these are Asian.

## The Christian presence
There are two issues which influence SCAG members faster than anything else. One is Asian immigrants and the other is vagrant alcoholics. Both have drastically affected the environment in which Spitalfields residents have to live. Rightly, they feel a burden has been placed on them which other districts do not have, and which a district like ours can ill afford on top of all its other difficulties as a run-down East End of London area. In this situation the Christian, because he worships the God of justice, does not shut his eyes to those things in the environment which are complained of; but at the same time sees that the immigrant is a human being too. Nothing he says or

does must deny the human dignity of the people around him, all of whom were made in the image of God.

The task of reconciliation and understanding is laid on the Christian's shoulders by his faith. Of course he finds plenty of other people in the social field who are equally concerned, but there is no doubt that a *Christian* presence makes a difference all its own. As one non-Christian social worker said to me of a churchless area, 'There is no presence there.' He believed this made a difference to the very atmosphere. Of course it must since a group of people who pray affects the very place it is in.

Jesus saw this function of his people quite clearly. He said in the Sermon on the Mount that we are the salt of the earth and the light of the world. He went on to spell this out. Salt, he said, gives savour. He was not speaking of preventing corruption but of giving things a salty tang. That is the kind of impact he wanted his followers to have on society. The source of our saltiness is God's Law and the Prophets.

## Making an impact

Of course there are problems when Christians exert an influence on the local community. When Spitalfields Crypt was opened for the re-habilitation of vagrant alcoholics, local folk took a dim view. They felt it would make the problem on the streets worse. Christian compassion demanded the response the Crypt founder, the Reverend Dennis Downham made, but it was contrary to how some ordinary people felt.

Perhaps one of the most direct ways of making an impact on the local community is by entering politics. One clergyman I know did this when asked to be an alderman. It meant his joining the Labour Party and accepting its discipline. There can be few politicians who have not at some time or another faced the clash between personal convictions and Party loyalty. The clergyman in question will find this to be true in full measure, I am sure. But meanwhile he can have a say in the central councils of the ruling party in his borough, so the 'salt' should be able to operate there.

Tenants' associations flourish or stagger along in many areas today. A Christian friend of mine is secretary of the one in his council flats. It is an opportunity to care for other people in the sort of practical ways that God expects us to do. Big organisations make for increasing dehumanisation and the local tenants' association is a way of off-setting this. Of course one is faced with the abrasive manner in which this world's children conduct their affairs so often. Some of the bitterness of public meetings can make one want to run away and keep out of it. But how will the 'salt' reach the food it is meant to savour if it stays in the cruet? A Christian in the right place at the right time can strengthen people of moderate persuasion and get things done peacefully.

## Protesting

This doesn't mean not protesting. In a Town Hall Clerks' strike which stopped our dustbins being emptied a Christian friend of mine led a procession there with pushchairs loaded with garbage. (One lady told me afterwards that she took some blowflies in a bottle and released them in the offices. A girl clerk said, 'There are a lot of flies in here,' to which our protester, not a church member I hasten to add, replied, 'They followed us from Spitalfields.') There is little doubt that the procession led to a speedy clearing of our dustbins!

Here and there, as Christians are engaged with other citizens in the affairs of the locality, the chance to witness to Christ and his laws does come. It may be done very clearly when we meet outside a local cinema to witness to the goodness of human love and sexuality against the pollution and exploitation going on inside. It may be when, as another Christian friend of mine has done, we get to work on the degrading material displayed in the newsagents. But in such cases we act *first* as citizens out of love for our neighbour. Gospel witness may or may not occur.

**Eddy Stride**

# 31
# How can a Christian be of most use to his trade union?

The question presupposes that the Christian is a member of his union. For some it is not as simple as that. The first question may well be, Can I as a Christian belong to a trade union? Will it spoil my witness, my separateness? Some would quote the words of St Paul, 'Do not be mismated with unbelievers;' and, 'Therefore come out from them and be separate from them, says the Lord, and touch nothing unclean' (2 Corinthians 6:14, 17). Read in this way the passage might seem to suggest that we should opt out of any organisation, profession, club, etc. to which non-Christians belong. But if the passage is carefully studied alongside such a story as the parable of the Good Samaritan (Luke 10:29–37) and the teaching of Jesus about salt and light in Matthew 5:13–16, I believe it will be seen that the general tenor of Scripture is on involvement, not on separation. Separation depends on a close walk with the Lord, not on external conditions.

## Getting involved
To be of any use in anything we must be involved. The chap on the touchline may spur the centre-forward on, but he can't score the goal. If he is watching the match on the TV in his front room he is even less use. A Christian trade unionist must be prepared to get involved. Paying one's dues is not enough. Salt is only useful if it is doing its job of flavouring and purifying.

Not everyone can become general secretary of his union, any more than every Anglican can be an archbishop. But in a union as in a church there is a minimum requirement for a faithful member.

If I can continue the analogy, the early Christians were told not to neglect to meet together, as was the habit of some (Hebrews 10:25). Today the same thing might well be said to trade unionists. One of our major weaknesses is the poor support given to branch meetings, shop floor meetings and district meetings. One even reads of strikes which involve thousands of people being continued because only hundreds have turned up to vote whether to return to work or not. Need I say that those who do turn up are the so-called militant minority, usually Communists or Marxists? Yet the Christians are called to be militant! Paul sees the Christian life as a battle and the Christian as a soldier. We find him using the army as an example again and again.

Christians certainly ought to attend their union meetings. This is not, I hasten to say, in order to oppose the Communists (the Christians may well find themselves voting and working with them on some issues) but to bring God's justice into the situation. The Bible has much to say about wages and conditions, employee/employer relationships, safety at work, work itself, and attitudes to it. Get hold of a good concordance and search out the truth of this. Ezekiel 34 will make a fair start.

## Holding office

We have differing gifts, and just as in a church situation some are called to hold office while others are not, so it is in the unions. I fear however that Christians are often afflicted with deafness when the Lord calls them to serve in trade unions. If you are asked to stand for office, make it a matter of prayer and ask your church and your Christian friends to pray for wisdom to be given to you. One of the great things about our faith is that we don't have to agree with what a person is doing before we can pray for him in the doing of it. If you do accept office as a branch secretary, money steward, or shop steward, you will need that prayer support; so keep people informed when you have important meetings or are faced with big decisions. You will also need to recognise that this sort of work will limit the time you can devote to the more conventional Christian spheres and activities.

## Those in favour say 'aye'

Even if holding office is not for you, voting most certainly is. Most union officials are elected by a small minority of the membership. Far-reaching decisions are often arrived at by a handful of members. So your vote is important. That means knowing what it's all about. Only too often at meetings I notice people looking round to see how those 'in the know' are voting before raising their hand. Equally I have quite often found myself voting for or against an issue and being a minority of one – only to be approached afterwards by someone who said, 'I agree with you, Frank, but what's the point when you're so out numbered?'.

If you have got an opinion, you ought to have the guts to show it. To have an opinion will mean discussing things with others, reading union journals, broadsheets, and newspapers, listening to radio and television debates, and picking out what is said by and about various candidates. Yes, it takes time, it means work, and sometimes it's boring. And yet I believe it is all part of loving one's neighbour as oneself.

## Giving support

Recently I spoke to our district secretary about the fact that after making a great display of strength on a particular issue, our union executive settled for a very small part of their claim. 'Well,' he said, 'I expect they looked over my shoulder for an army and found it had deserted.' It was true. What they were asking for had little support from the rank and file. Members had no stomach for the fight, and the leader knew it.

I need hardly say that there are limits to backing our leadership. The apostles were quite firm with the early Christians that they must obey all lawful authority because it is ordained of God. In this country trade unions are a lawful authority, protected by Parliament and the courts. Yet when Peter and John were ordered by the lawful Jewish authority (the rulers of the people and elders) not to speak or teach in the name of Jesus, they flatly refused to obey them (Acts 4:19, 20). So our final authority is God. We may at some point have to stand against our leadership if its decisions are clearly contrary to God's laws. This is something which could only be done after much thought and prayer. It could be costly in terms of employment, friendship and even health. We follow one who said it would be so. It was for him.

**Frank Deeks**

**Further reading**

*Shop Floor Christianity* Frank Deeks (IVP)
*The Christian in Industrial Society* Frederick Catherwood (Tyndale Press)
*Built as a City* David Sheppard (Hodder & Stoughton)
*An Introduction to British Trade Unions* Ben Hulberman (Penguin)

# 32
# How far should our conscience dictate our social behaviour?

'So always let your conscience be your guide.' That is how the old song put it and it is fine up to a point. But it is not the whole story. We must be clear what we mean when we speak of 'conscience,' because a Christian understanding of it differs from that suggested by the way people often speak. 'My conscience is clear' implies a final verdict of innocence; but is that necessarily true? Is it invariably infallible? Do we all possess this kind of inbuilt moral compass? People sometimes say of someone, 'He has got no conscience at all.'

Although the actual word only occurs a few times in the Bible, mainly in Paul's letters, the idea is present throughout. 'A pure heart' implies much the same thing (Psalm 24:4). This purity of heart depends upon an awareness of good and evil. Consequently for the Israelite the observance of the law was the guarantee of a clear conscience, because here God had shown what was required of man. But even this was not enough. Job was convinced of his righteousness (Job 27:6) until he came face to face with God (Job 42:5, 6). Here is something much more profound. The ultimate secret of a clear conscience is closeness to God. Outward observance of the law is not enough – the Lord looks upon the heart. Thought and motive count with God as well as outward behaviour. This was what the Pharisees had failed to understand (eg Matthew 15:2) and it was the turning-point for Saul of Tarsus when he reflected on the command, 'You shall not covet' (Romans 7:7).

**Limitations of conscience**

This is not to say that only those who belong to God's people and possess his written law have an operative conscience. Paul explains that Gentiles too show some awareness of God's law and their conscience bears witness to the fact (Romans 2:14–16). All men, made in God's image, have a moral sense given by God, however much they may abuse it. By itself it is inadequate. It needs the further enlightenment of what God has revealed in the law. Still more, under the new covenant, this law of God is to be re-written on men's hearts by the Spirit (Hebrews 8:10). By this means the conscience is enlivened and man is empowered by the Holy Spirit to observe the spirit of God's law as well as the letter. So Paul can say confidently, 'God is my witness,' in order to support what he is claiming: his conscience is clear. Uniquely in Jesus we find that absolute purity of conscience that only sinlessness and total obedience can provide (John 8:29).

From what has been said we can see that conscience is not by itself an autonomous and infallible guide for our social behaviour. My conscience may not be accusing me when I deserve it, because I am not fully aware of God's law or am out of touch with the living God. But every man has a conscience and a duty not to act against it.

'Pangs' of conscience accurately express the biblical teaching about it, for this pain is an internal effect of God's wrath against sin (Romans 1:18). This is the pain felt after the commission of a sin; but, as in a game when the light flashes on after you have missed the target, so conscience only registers *after* failure. Its role is negative, indicating that some transgression has occurred. Of course it may register also in anticipation as the 'mind' toys with the possibility of a certain course of action, but the New Testament distinguishes these two things (Romans 2:14, 15). While the 'conscience' is basically negative and retrospective, the 'mind' is able also to deliberate on choices beforehand.

**An enlightened conscience**

On many matters of social behaviour there is clear and explicit direction in the Bible: for the Christian the right course is obvious. But what about those innumerable areas where there is no precise instruction in the Bible? As we progress in the Christian life our conscience should become more sensitive to what is right because it is better informed. We are not to be 'squeezed into the world's mould'

(Romans 12:2). The principles of conduct laid down in the Bible change our attitudes as we begin more to see things through Christ's eyes. One might imagine that this means that we will tend always to become increasingly rigid and inflexible, but that is not the case. Whilst our moral standards ought to be continually rising, we should also be discovering a new liberty – a freedom from man-made rules and superstitions by which we were once enslaved.

Now this kind of slavery is much more common amongst Christians than we usually care to admit. The man who has been delivered from this Paul calls 'strong,' but the man with a 'weak' conscience has not yet achieved this understanding and freedom (Romans 15:1, 1 Corinthians 8:7). Therefore, as a person matures spiritually, so his conscience may disallow some things that once were unquestioned and permit other things that previously were disapproved. So, if conscience develops in this way, it will never provide by itself a consistent pattern of guidance for my social behaviour. My own attitudes will change over the years concerning some of these greyer areas of conduct.

## Respect for others

There is another factor here also. I have no right to lay down the law for anyone else beyond the clear teaching of Scripture, any more than I should allow someone to do the same for me. To our own master we stand or fall. Paul is insistent that our own liberty and enlightenment should never be allowed to damage someone else's conscience. To ride rough-shod over their moral sensitivity, even if it be ill-informed and the work of a 'weak' conscience, is to flout the higher law of love for my Christian brother. Love is superior to liberty. My new-found freedom must never be allowed to harm the conscience of another for whom Christ died. Consequently I may find it necessary at times to deny myself certain liberties that I firmly believe are fully permissible for myself for the sake of my 'weaker brother,' lest I encourage him to act against his conscience to his own detriment (1 Corinthians 8:13).

Take, for example, the question of smoking. Is it right for me? Obviously the Bible has nothing direct to say. It is expensive – but so are many other little indulgences. It is bad for the health – but so, we are told, are all animal fats. It is habit-forming – but so is tea-drinking. 'It is anti-social' – but its supporters would claim the opposite. You can argue the toss endlessly. In the end each one must decide honestly for himself without writing off those who may disagree. The same with drinking. Drunkenness is a terrible scourge, but wine is said to 'make glad the heart of man.' Can I control my own appetites? Could my example lead others astray? Or would a very negative attitude on my part unnecessarily confirm people's identification of Christianity with moral taboos? Let each one of us be fully persuaded in his own mind. And my loving concern for other people should keep me open to a change in my own behaviour in a different social situation.

A final word of warning. If we repeatedly act against our conscience, it will cease to function as it ought. It can become defiled (Titus 1:15) and even cauterised to the extent of complete in-sensitivity (1 Timothy 4:2). That is to travel in the reverse direction of God's purpose, for he wishes us to live so close to him that our conscience is clear and uncondemning. But even then, when no pangs are felt, the Christian knows that the final judge of his conduct is not his conscience but God (1 Corinthians 4:4).

**Julian Charley**

# 33
# If life's a gamble, why not have a flutter?

The evidence is all around us. Scarcely a shopping parade does not boast at least one bookmakers. Posters on station hoardings urge greater investments in Premium Bonds and newspapers regularly announce the lucky numbers drawn by 'Ernie.' Pictures of smiling pools winners feed the instant-wealth fantasies indulged in by thousands every weekend.

Gambling is a national industry of enormous size and complexity. It also raises emphatically a moral question. First, a definition: 'Gambling is an agreement between two parties, the main purpose of which is to affect the transfer of something of value (cash or goods) from one to the other on the basis of the uncertain outcome of an event over which they have no control and which, before the agreement was made, did not constitute a risk to either, so that one party will gain and the other lose.'

## Sorting things out
That may seem a long and involved definition for a simple enough word, but such elaboration is necessary if the subject is to be rescued from facile superficiality. Read the definition again, slowly, and you will see that it sorts out the chaff from the wheat – or perhaps, more appropriately, the wild oats.

On this understanding of the meaning of the word the phrase 'life is a gamble' dissolves into meaninglessness. So, too, do suggestions that insurance or stock exchange dealings are a gamble (though there are circumstances in which the latter can sometimes qualify). On the other hand the placing of bets on horses, dogs, an increasingly wide range of sports, political elections and even the appointment of archbishops is quite clearly gambling. So, too, are football pools, those games of chance usually associated with the casinos and any lottery in which the prizes are awarded simply on the luck of the draw (that includes Premium Bonds, the interest forfeited being the stake).

Somewhere in the grey area between the two clearly defined groups come games and activities such as Bingo, Spot-the-ball contests and some amusement arcade machines where a minimal amount of skill is required of those taking part, mild family wagers over domestic trivialities, participation in raffles for good causes where the desire to be a benefactor vastly outweighs the profit motive, and the occasional flutter undertaken primarily to add colour to an otherwise drab existence, as someone has put it, somewhat patronisingly.

## Personal behaviour

Gambling poses for the Christian a moral question at two levels: personal behaviour and social significance. So far as the first is concerned it is more a question of what the Bible does not say than what it does say. Within its pages only four ways of obtaining money are commended: working for it, selling something for it, receiving it as a present or as interest on an investment. It is not unreasonable therefore to deduce that obtaining money by gambling is alien to the purposes of God. More decisively the Ten Commandments, though they do not say 'You shall not bet,' do say 'You shall not covet,' and gambling as already defined is quite clearly a transgression of the tenth commandment. However, it must be remembered that covetousness has many faces; moral censoriousness about 'speck'-like gambling should be more than matched by concern about the 'planks' of avarice, greed, envy and lust which often restrict our own vision.

Gambling is not a subject upon which many church leaders have pronounced with distinction or great frequency. One of the best quotes on record comes from Archbishop William Temple:

Gambling challenges that view of life which the Christian Church exists to uphold and extend. Its glorification of mere chance is a denial of the divine order of nature. To risk money haphazardly is to disregard the insistence of the Church in every age of living faith, that possessions are a trust, and that men must account to God for their use. The persistent appeal to covetousness is fundamentally opposed to the unselfishness which was taught by Jesus ... The attempt to make profit out of the inevitable loss of others is the antithesis of that love of one's neighbour on which our Lord insisted.

How should Christians apply these stirring words to their moral behaviour? Clearly they should have no part in 'pure' gambling, that is, games of chance for money, lotteries, football pools and betting in all its forms. That rules out Premium Bonds and the office sweepstake, but what about that other hardy annual, the raffle held in aid of a worthy cause? It is easy enough to say, 'Offer a straight donation to the cause instead,' but less easy to put it into practice and for that reason such a response can be taken by critics to be an indication of mean-mindedness. A simpler way to retain both integrity and credibility is to buy a ticket and publicly tear it up to demonstrate disinterest in winning a prize.

As to whether churches or Christian organisations should raise funds by any of these methods, the same principles apply. To use means so dubious, however worthy the cause, is at best a case of justifying the lesser of two evils, at worst to run the risk of the means being incompatible with the end.

## The social issue

Gambling as a social issue is very much a Cinderella so far as the church is concerned, registering several degrees below poverty, racialism, pornography, alcoholism, homelessness and other social ills. Cold statistics (which in any case would be out-of-date by the time this appeared in print) can easily mask the individual human situations in which gamblers often find themselves. At whatever level the gambling industry is judged it is very difficult to justify. In terms of results, the happiness accruing to the handful of winners must pale by comparison with the accumulated frustration of the majority who lose. Does any other industry of comparable size contribute so little in terms of productivity? At a time when the nation's resources need to be concentrated on the production of real wealth it seems madness to waste so much manpower, materials, time and effort on unproductive gambling. There may well be a case for the redistribution of wealth, but not this way, surely.

Gambling on its present scale has the added disadvantage of helping to put the skids under hard work and thrift, with most people preferring to go for the chance of a quick, undemanding reward.

There are sufficient cases known where gambling has led to dishonesty and hardship involving family and friends to suggest that society should start taking its damaging consequences much more seriously than at present.

The proper Christian response to the moral questions posed by gambling is to take every opportunity to draw attention to its antisocial effects, to oppose moves aimed at enlarging and institutionalising the gambling industry, and to support legislation which seeks to reduce the damage it does. At the personal level Christians should seek to free themselves of every trace of that covetousness which in almost every form of gambling is the root cause.

**John Capon**

# 34
# Are there any limits to Christian freedom?

'Free,' 'freedom,' 'liberty' are heady terms, conjuring up notions of the French Revolution, the ending of the slave trade, and, in more recent history, movements to bring about a greater measure of self-determination and equality for oppressed peoples. To have a part in a freedom movement appeals to many young people, and one admires their altruistic motive.

## Jewish history
Release from the bondage of Egypt is a major theme in the Old Testament history of Israel. The cry of the slaves was heard by God, who responded by sending Moses to be their deliverer. After a series of disasters the king of Egypt was willing to let them go; indeed such was the distress of the population that they urged the Israelites to get out as quickly as possible. At the crucial moment a way was opened for them to cross on foot land which had previously been sea-covered, and they found themselves delivered from the Egyptians and out of reach of their power. They were free.

But the God who had delivered them had claims on them, and at Sinai they accepted that this was so. 'All that the Lord has spoken we will do and be obedient' (Exodus 24:7). They owed it to the God who had set them free to live in such a way as to please him, and that meant keeping his commandments. The same is true for every Christian. He owes it to the one who has bought his freedom to live in such a way as to please him.

The question of freedom was an important issue among the Jews of

Jesus's day. Despite invasions, conquests and humiliation they reckoned proudly that they had never been slaves to any man (John 8:33). Words of Josephus bear this out: 'Long ago, my brave men, we determined neither to serve the Romans nor any other save God, for he alone is man's true and righteous Lord ... we preferred death to slavery' (*Wars of the Jews* vii, 323). In conversation with Jesus this was the concept of freedom they always had in mind, whereas Jesus spoke of another aspect of the subject. They were not listening sufficiently closely to catch his meaning and so there was constant misunderstanding. Jesus had in mind not political bondage but personal bondage to self-centred thoughts and deeds which set fixed limits on the moral freedom of the individual. So long as a person is happy to accept himself as he is, he is unaware of the extent to which he has forfeited his freedom, but let him try to transform himself so that he fulfils even his own ideals and he will find himself powerless to bring about any lasting change. It follows that he is a slave, unable to bring about his release.

## Christ the Liberator

It is such a release that Jesus has in mind when he says, 'If you continue in my word, then you are truly my disciples; and you shall know the truth and the truth will make you free' (John 8:31, 32). This verse brings us to the heart of the Christian concept of freedom. First and foremost it is liberation from a slavery that is so habitual that for much of the time we are unconscious of it. The extent of its hold on the entire personality is glimpsed only when the word of truth of which Jesus speaks begins its liberating work in a person's life. Then he begins to realise just how limited he has been. Freedom is seen to be nothing less than salvation. As the one who is entirely free from sin Jesus is the true liberator of others (John 8:36).

It follows, however, that those whom he frees must, like him, do only those things that are in harmony with the Father's will and pleasure. Looked at in terms of a human understanding of freedom, this qualification of the concept may be unacceptable; but this is the meaning of Christian freedom. Only when a person has been set free in this way does he begin to live as God intended he should, knowing in his experience the 'glorious liberty of the children of God' (Romans 8:21).

The use of that phrase of Paul leads into his treatment of this theme, for he also agreed that apart from Christ, people live in bondage, even if they are largely unaware of it. They know that something is wrong, that some malaise affects the whole of life, and this Paul identifies as sin reigning in human lives and working towards certain death (Romans 5:21). They are in bondage to sin (Romans 6:6, 13), but are now being offered their release in order to become slaves of righteousness.

### Free—for what?

The *limitations* of the freedom they are being offered are thus made very plain. It is a freedom not to do as they please, but a glorious freedom to do only what is right, which he later expresses as freedom to become God's bondservants (Romans 6:22), released from fear, called his sons, and as such, due to inherit untold riches in Christ (Romans 8). No small part of the wonder Paul expresses in the fact that the requirements of the law will be fulfilled in those who believe (Romans 8:3). They are not saved by law keeping, but having found salvation, they fulfil the law and in so doing find God's service to be perfect freedom.

As a pastor, Paul saw that a Christian's freedom has to be limited by one more factor. Outside the absolute demands which God makes on all his children there are neutral areas in which the individual Christian has freedom of choice. He may, for instance, marry or remain single, work for his living or accept support as a servant of the Gospel; he is also free to eat whatever food is put before him. It may be, however, that he finds himself among Christians who, because of their past life, have scruples about some aspects of behaviour.

The example Paul himself gives (1 Corinthians 8) of eating food which had been used as an offering to idols would still be meaningful in some parts of the world. To someone who has been accustomed to think of an idol as a god to be reckoned with it would be scandalous to eat anything that had been offered in a temple. In that case a fellow Christian is to respect the difficulties of such a person and refuse to eat that food. A recent convert from Hinduism or Buddhism would shun a temple like the plague, whereas the visitor from the West would see no problem in going to see what went on there. He too would have to be careful to give no offence to local Christians. The person who has been an alcoholic will not be helped if he finds himself expected to drink alcohol. It could be his downfall. For this reason the Christian, out of love for his fellow believer, will forego alcohol in order to help his friend.

Unquestionably, therefore, there are limitations on a Christian's liberty. He is free to do good, to be generous-hearted, to be forgiving, thoughtful for others, forgetful of self interest; in short, to be loving. He is not free to indulge in the corresponding vices; but then as a Christian he no longer wants to indulge in them, and when he lapses into his old ways he hates himself for so doing. In other words he has become a new person, truly happy when he is fulfilling his new nature and miserable when he is not. The limitations imposed on the Christian's freedom by God's demands are therefore more apparent than real. In a glad acceptance of these demands he finds true liberty.

**Joyce Baldwin**

**Further reading**
*Free to do Right* David Field (IVP)
*Choose Freedom* Michael Green (IVP)

# 35
# Why does truth matter?

When Jesus stood before Pilate he said, 'My task is to bear witness to the truth. For this was I born; for this I came into the world, and all who are not deaf to truth listen to my voice' (John 18:37 NEB).

Pilate replied in words that have become famous and are often echoed, 'What is truth?' This question is more pertinent than ever today because there are many who would agree that truth matters, but they could not agree on what is truth. There is a simple and important explanation of this situation: we live in a post-Christian world. That is not saying that once Western society was made up only of Christians, but rather that Christianity was the norm on which society was based. Even a person who was not a professing Christian was aware of this basis. A belief in God, and particularly in a God who has revealed himself to us and who shows us how to live, means that there are absolute standards to live by and that we can know absolute though not exhaustive truth.

## Absolute or relative

In our society today God is no longer seen as relevant. He is dead – if he ever existed at all apart from being an illusion, or a psychological prop. This has very far-reaching implications. If there is no personal God creating us and our universe then we are products of chance and of no more significance than the animals or inanimate objects. We have no value. Our only meaning or purpose in life, if such a concept is possible, is to survive and to make our survival as pleasant and painless as can be.

In this situation it is not possible to have any absolute values. There is nothing from which to derive them. Everything becomes relative –

and this includes truth. Without an authority outside ourselves, how can we measure such a value? It simply becomes 'your truth' or 'my truth.' This is not necessarily a new idea formed to reflect the mood of our age; it's just that it has become the overriding viewpoint now.

For example, there is a piece of writing found on the wall of Old St Paul's Church, Baltimore, which dates back to the seventeenth century. It starts off, 'Go placidly amidst the noise and haste' and is more often known as *Desiderata*. It has been released on record with a music backing several times, and it says, 'Speak *your truth* quietly and clearly.' I shall quote another piece from this later on to show that this is seen as a relative statement; but it is sufficient to say at this point that one of the reasons *Desiderata* is particularly popular in our society is that it is 'religious' in a vague sense while at the same time undermining the whole basis of Christianity.

## Changing values
So 'What is truth?' is answered in our society by saying 'Whatever you make it.' Once society had very definite values, even if it could not keep them. This led to an illusion of permanence. Now we are in a world where values shift and change all the time. This is illustrated very well in the film *O Lucky Man*. There Alan Price sings a song called *Changes* to the tune of *What a Friend we have in Jesus*. It shows the shift of emphasis in the hymn. No longer is it a song which shows that one can have absolute confidence in God. Instead, it has become a hymn to change, stating that no one knows what is going on.

It is a wholly fatalistic idea. We are here one day and then gone, but the world carries on – and that is all there is. The theme of the film is that there is no meaning in life, but you cannot exist at that level, so if you can find a reason to live, or a reason to keep you happy, then hang on to it. It does not matter what it is, it does not matter if it's true or false (those terms are meaningless as we have seen), you're a lucky man if you have found a reason to go on living.

The same idea is illustrated in some of John Lennon's songs. In 1971 he was singing *Gimme some truth*, but by 1974 he was singing *Whatever gets you thru the night* which is stating the same things as *O Lucky Man*. Whatever you can find to get you through your life – that's all right. It doesn't matter what it is, or whether it is right or wrong. It's whatever gets you through the night, whatever helps you make the most of survival.

So the concepts of right and wrong, truth and falsehood, are shifting and changing in our society because there is no belief in an absolute God. And so it becomes whatever turns you on, whatever keeps you happy. This is the new religion. And the ultimate blasphemy is to tell someone that you know the answer, and that they are wrong. This is amazing arrogance! After all, it is only *your* truth, as opposed to *their* truth.

This is why a conversation between people of totally different religious viewpoints or philosophies of life can run like this: 'Hey, man, I'm into Jesus!' 'Oh, far out, I'm into Buddha!' And each can accept the other. There is no sense of conflict because underlying everything anyway is the assumption that there is nothing that is right and wrong, and no meaning, so it does not matter what you believe as long as it helps you get by. You may be into eastern mysticism, political ideas, drugs or Jesus. It's whatever turns you on.

## The Christian concept of truth

Back then to *Desiderata*: 'Therefore be at peace with God *whatever you conceive him to be.*' That is why this statement is so popular in our society. This is why for the Christian today the concept of truth is more important than ever before. First, he has to show that he believes in truth in a different way. In other words in such a way that if one viewpoint contradicts another, one is true, and therefore the other must be false. But he has to show that this concept of truth can be traced back to the existence of a loving and personal God who has revealed himself to us in Jesus Christ. Jesus came to bear witness to the truth, and indeed he declared himself to be truth.

If this is to be a meaningful statement to our generation we have to show in what sense we are using the word 'truth.' It is not a relative, shifting, all-embracing concept, but it is a narrow and well-defined concept because it comes from God who has created us, and whom we can know. It is not enough for a Christian today to say to someone, 'Become a Christian because then you'll be happy,' for that puts Christianity on the level of another trip. It is not enough to say, 'Become a Christian because Christianity works.' It's important that it does work, but again lots of things 'work.' Almost all religions have their miracles. If you accept a philosophical or religious viewpoint, however unreasonable, it will quite probably help you to be happy and things will 'work' for you.

But the most important point for the Christian to communicate today is that there is such a thing as truth, and that people should believe in Christ because Christianity is true. It can be seen to be true by looking at our world, and thereby verifying the truths of the Bible. It follows from this that honesty must be an integral part of the Christian lifestyle – if we are committed to truth. It also follows that we can have great confidence in the power of God's word and its ability to speak to each situation when we recognise that this and this alone reveals the truth about us, our world and our Creator.

## A liberating experience

Discovery of the truth that there is a God and that we can know him is a liberating experience. Jesus said: 'If you dwell within the revelation I have brought, you are indeed my disciples; you shall know the truth, and the truth shall set you free' (John 8:31, 32). First, of course, this destroys the lie that man is of no significance. He is of enormous value because he has been made 'in God's image.' It helps us to understand our own value and that of our neighbour. Second, it explains the problems and confusions of our world because we see that man is away from God; so it helps us to understand our world, and the position of man within it. Third, it gives us a new way of life that is truly liberating because we live within the context and in the knowledge of our Creator, thereby discovering from him and his truth revealed in scripture how to find fulfilment.

The concept of truth goes totally against the whole mood of our Western society today with its assertion of absolute and permanent values and its confident statement that there is a God and he is most clearly revealed in his Son, Jesus Christ. To many this will appear as arrogance; but how can it appear as anything else if any assertion that one thing is right and another is wrong is not acceptable?

## Truth is a lovely tune

*(song lyric)*

Truth is a lovely tune,
I've heard that tune before;
It's playing down the centuries,
It'll play for evermore.

But only those with ears to hear
Can hear the sound it makes,
And only those with eyes to see
Follow the road it takes.

And stemming from its melody
Come love and justice too;
But those who'd sing the song of truth
Must learn to suffer too.

Truth is a two-edged sword,
It wounds and causes pain;
But truth is a healing sound,
It brings new life again.

And Jesus on his cross of wood,
Eyes are filled with pain;
'I am truth' was what he'd said –
And Truth rose again.

**Garth Hewitt**

### Further reading
*The God Who is There* Francis Schaeffer (Hodder & Stoughton)
*Escape from Reason* Francis Schaeffer (IVP)
*The Dust of Death* Os Guinness (IVP)

# 36

# Has the church in the West been guilty of making Christianity unacceptable to other cultures?

**The white man's burden**

Taking time to skim through some popular missionary literature of the Victorian era will force us to admit that this has frequently been the case. Especially during the colonial era, which coincided with the modern missionary movement, western civilization was inseparably intertwined with the gospel so that some countries within 'Christendom' tended to regard themselves almost as God's gift to the universe. It was naively thought that their material prosperity was the result of God's special blessing; a reward for their piety.

Along with the gospel was offered the European and North American cultural heritage, which represented in the eyes of the missionaries the outworking of the gospel. As a consequence, national cultures tended to be discounted or undervalued. There were, however, notable exceptions among the missionary ranks, and in all our criticisms we must remember that the missionaries despite their shortcomings were more sensitive than their fellow countrymen, who were motivated by commercial interests.

**Dangers today**

If we now need, with the perspective of history, to correct the

**156**

triumphalism and idealism which marked the missionary movement until the First World War had its humbling effect, we also need to guard against today's current of cynicism, which regards the missionary movement as a huge con-trick designed to sanction and support the West's colonial expansion. To write off mission in these terms is to fly in the face of the evidence. The missionary movement was not the result of the church management's policy decision to initiate an export drive. It was carried out in the face of the apathy and even open hostility of the ecclesiastical establishment. In addition, not a few colonial administrators regarded missionaries as a danger to themselves and a disturbing influence in their territory, and did all in their power to obstruct missionary endeavours.

In the development of mission mistakes galore have been made, some of them with tragic consequences. The same can be said about the development of medicine. And as with medicine, alongside the errors there have been many remarkable achievements. The missionary movement has established Christian churches around the world, so that today there are far more Christians outside the old boundaries of 'Christendom' than within it. If missionary expansion had been dependent upon colonial influence, we would have expected the churches to fold up with the assumption of independence. In fact quite the reverse happened – the growing edge of Christianity is increasingly to be found outside Europe and North America. In some instances the Church is flourishing despite a hostile environment. Additionally, we must not forget that it was the missionary movement which introduced, manned and trained national personnel for the medical and educational services which the newly-independent nations have rightly taken over.

Today there is a far greater sensitivity to cultural values in non-Western civilization. Many missionaries, trained in anthropology and sociology, are seeking to interpret the gospel in local cultural settings. National Christians and their missionary colleagues are sensitive to detect areas in which Western Christians have distorted the gospel through addition, subtraction and division.

## Addition
Western Christians have added to the gospel attitudes of mind and patterns of behaviour which they have made part of the package. Their attitudes to work, their stress on economic self-sufficiency and their regard for possessions have bred materialistic attitudes. In some

areas, mission has been promoted with the technique dependence characteristic of big business. For instance Latin America's Evangelism-in-Depth programme has come in for a great deal of criticism on account of its dependence on success-guaranteed methods, high-powered missionary technocrats, and stereotyped message content. Latin American protest has led to an entirely new approach, with nationals determining the programme so that it is appropriate for a given area.

In some countries becoming a Christian almost entails becoming a 'foreigner' in the eyes of the people, as they see the convert beginning to express himself in Western thought forms, dress differently (in India preferring a suit to a dhoti or a dress for a sari), and use unfamiliar forms of music. The devotional content of church services is still largely dependent on North American and European piety. An electric or pipe organ may be installed in church as a mark of prestige even though such instruments are virtually unknown in the country at large.

## Subtraction

Western missionaries have tended to stress the individual and private aspects of religion to the detriment of the corporate and community emphases of the cultures in which they work. They have also been blinkered with regard to the socio-political dimensions of the gospel, so that Latin American theologians, evangelical as well as liberal, accuse them of preaching a truncated and inadequate gospel. In their social aid programmes, the Westerners have in the past concentrated on the alleviation of symptoms, rather than investigating and exposing the causes of poverty, disease and ignorance. Also, their stress on the theoretical and the abstract has suppressed the emotional and non-rational dimensions of true communion with God and encounter with fellow believers.

## Division

Through their highly individualistic evangelical approach and stress on the need for personal decisions for Christ, missionaries from Europe and North America have sometimes caused needless divisions within families, and alienated individual families from their village communities. Such divisions may result from the differences the gospel makes, but in some instances much conflict could have been avoided by a more sensitive and patient approach. In certain cultures the decision will be a family step rather than an individual one, and in village life a people's movement may occur. Anyone coming to another society needs to be sensitive to the cultural as well as the theological obstacles to faith.

A further serious aspect is the way that Protestant missions have divided the body of Christ into umpteen denominations. There are over 250 in Brazil, and in many countries around the world you will find Northern and Southern Baptists, which has nothing to do with their location in the country, but to the split in Baptist ranks caused by the American Civil War!

## Reversing the trend

Yet there are many encouraging signs that David is throwing off the cumbersome Western armour. National church unity schemes, third-world understandings of the gospel, worship enriched by local culture, new patterns of ministry, and spontaneous growth all provide clear evidences of life.

The church overseas are also doing a service to the church in the West by reminding Christians there of dimensions of the gospel which they have conveniently forgotten, and by rescuing them from their uncritical local attitudes. The presence of such people in the West will provide some much needed colour to the 'White man's religion,' so that it will become less of a mirror reflecting the attitude of Western society and more of a light bringing the challenge of the gospel of the Kingdom of God.

**Eddie Gibbs**